David Anderson

The Complete Guide to
Teddy Bear Puppies

Everything to Know about Finding, Raising & Loving Your Teddy

Contents

Chapter 16

Chapter 17

Chapter 18

CHAPTER 1

SHIH TZU

BICHON FRISE

TEDDY BEAR PUPPIES:
A HISTORY OF THE CROSS-BREED

The term "Teddy Bear Puppy" is most commonly used when referring to the cross breed of a Bichon Frise and a Shih Tzu. This cross breed is also known as a Shichon or a Zuchon, but the term "Teddy Bear Puppy" or "Teddy Bear Dog" has become the most commonly used term in describing the breed over the past 10 years.

The exact origins of the Teddy Bear puppy are not well documented. Since both the parent breeds have been common in America since the mid 1900's, there have most likely been accidental cross breedings between a Bichon and a Shih Tzu at different times over the past 50-70 years. These original Teddy Bears were likely just referred to as mutts since the popularity of cross-bred designer dogs didn't really start until the late 1980's and early 1990's.

Other cross-breeds have tried to garner the name "Teddy Bear Dog" in the past, however, none have stuck like the Bichon/Shih Tzu cross.

Early Types of Teddy Bear Puppies

On May 20th 1991 in the Sun-Journal of Lewiston, Maine an article appeared documented the efforts of a private dog breeder named Steven M. Brown to create a "Teddy Bear Dog" that exhibited the characteristics of a cuddly teddy bear. Mr. Brown aimed to achieve this ideal dog, dubbed a "Charlie Bear" by cross-breeding a Soft-Coated Wheaten Terrier and the Portuguese Water dog. The goal was to create a mild tempered companion dog that would make the ideal pet for a family. However, the name, and cross-breed didn't stick and the "Charlie Bear" quietly faded away.

The late 1990's exhibit the earliest records of a reference to the name Shichon or Zuchon. An article appearing on the website dogpage.us in 1997 is the first internet reference to the cross-breed. This srticle served as a brief summary of the basics of the breed and referenced both the Shih Tzu and Bichon Frise parentage of the dogs. However, the article contained no mention of the breeds history or orgins, which remain unclear to this day.

Where Did the Cross-Breed Come From?

Even some of the most well-recognized individuals in the teddy bear community can't pin down the breeds exact origins. Ashley Lack, who runs the incredibly popular Facebook group: Shichons, isn't positive on where or when the breed actually started:

"I'm honestly not exactly sure what the breeds origins are, besides that the two parents would make a great puppy because of the Bichon & Shit-tzu's positive characteristics. :)

Some Shichons have been bred as therapy dogs. They can serve as therapy dogs for children with Autism, be seizure-alert dogs, or work as service dogs. They also were bred because of their non-shedding coat, which is good for people with allergies. I feel once people have found out about their personalities though; they've grown in popularity (especially in the last year) because they're such great companions!"

Three Names, One Dog: Shichons, Zuchons, and Teddy Bears

The cross-breed maintained the name Shichon, and less commonly "Zuchon", through the 1990's until breeders started referring to them as "Teddy Bear Puppies" starting in 2003. The cute name was very memorable and acted as a great marketing tool for breeders. The term "Teddy Bear Puppy" is a lot easier to remember and more fun to say than "Shichon" or "Zuchon".

During the mid 2000's the breed began to gain more and more popularity, starting in the Midwest: Wisconsin, Minnesota, Illinois, and Iowa and slowly spreading across the country.

As the breed continued to gain fans, the name also gained massive popularity and by the year 2006 "Teddy Bear Dog" had over twice as many Google searches as both the terms "Shichon" and "Zuchon" combined.

In fact, in an apparent effort to capitalize on the growing popularity of the name, a small breeder in Wisconsin attempted to start the "American Teddy Bear Association" in 2003 and claimed to be the only one authorized to sell the dogs under the name "Teddy

Bear Puppy". The breeders even went as far as to sell "franchises" to other dog breeders granting them the rights to use the name "Teddy Bear Puppy". However, in 2007 the Wisconsin Division of Securities quickly ruled that the sale of these unregistered franchises was not legal and ordered them to be revoked.

Still, the name "Teddy Bear Puppy" has continued to gain popularity and acceptance across the United States over the past 20 years. Now there are teddy bear puppies in virtually all 50 states and breeders located in over 35 states.

There are also several less common names used to refer to the breed: Fuzzy Wuzzy pups, Rag Doll dogs, and Ewaoks. These terms are usually region specific and haven't gained the widespread use like "teddy bear puppies" has.

Growing in Popularity

The breed is still most popular in the Midwest, with over 27% of all visitors to Miniteddybearpuppies.com coming from Wisconsin, Illinois, Minnesota, and Iowa. However, both coasts have also embraced the teddy bear puppy as New York and California are the 4th and 8th ranked states with the most visitors.

One thing is for sure, as time goes on the teddy bear puppy continues to gain more and more popularity. It wouldn't be unreasonable to expect that in 15-20 years it will become as common and popular as almost any dog breed in the world.

CHAPTER 2

WHAT IS A TEDDY BEAR PUPPY?

As a mix between the Bichon Frise and Shih Tzu breeds, the Teddy Bear Puppy has many of the same characteristics of its parents. Soft, cuddly, and hypo-allergenic, many of its owners believe it is the perfect dog.

Ashley Lack, creator of the Shichons Facebook group, agrees:

"Shichons are the most amazing pups. They care deeply about their families, following them room-to-room, even to "check up" on them! They love to play, & when properly trained, will only chew their toys.

Shichons also have this intelligence in their eyes I've never seen before looking into another animal's eyes. They really, truly understand what you are saying when you speak to them. An example of this with my 7 year-old Shichon, Ella is the fact that my family & I started spelling the word "walk" when we were ready to go & she figured out what that meant! They are highly trainable, picking up tricks very quickly. Ella can fetch, wave, dance, sit, lay, sit up (on her back legs), high five, & shake. She also has great instincts.

When I became very ill with kidney problems, she was a gentle, constant companion! Many members of Shichons note that their dog has done the same thing while they've been feeling under the weather or are upset. Overall, they are just a perfect family dog!"

Why Are They Called "Teddy Bears"

The term "Teddy Bear" has become popular with the breed not only because it sounds cute, but because when the dogs are young, they actually resemble a Teddy Bear! This is mostly due to their small size, delicate features, fluffy coat, large eyes, and general resemblance to a stuffed teddy bear.

Many owners have also noticed that their facial features and longer hair makes many older teddy bear puppies resemble an "Ewok" from the popular Star Wars franchise. In fact many of the cute "Dog Ewok" Halloween costumes you may have seen are actually teddy bear puppies. Because of this uncanny resemblance, a few people have even come to refer to the dogs as Ewoak puppies.

AKC Recognition

Teddy Bears are not an officially recognized breed of dog by the AKC. However, it is possible that with several more generations of breeding and growing popularity they will be able to gain acceptance. If and when that happens it will most likely be under the name "Shichon" or Zuchon" as it seems unlikely the tight-collared members of the AKC would ever consider a dog named a "Teddy Bear Puppy"

The Physical Characteristics

Teddy Bear dogs can grow to be up to 20 lbs., but usually weigh between 11-16 when fully grown. They can be a mixture of different colors including white, black, and many different shades of brown. This adds to their appeal amongst dog owners because two Teddy Bears almost never look completely similar.

Teddy Bears are extremely loyal dogs and love physical contact. It is not unusual for a Teddy to take a midday nap on your lap, or at your feet. They usually get along very well with other pets, especially other dogs, and are very good with small children. In fact, they started out being bred as therapy dogs for children with disabilities. Their mild temperament makes them the perfect companion for just about anyone. They do not typically bark, but they will if they sense danger, or when someone new enters their house for the first time.

Most teddy bears are also hypo-allergenic, which makes them perfect for anyone with allergies. They have typically been bred to produce very little dander, so even if you are allergic to most dogs, a Teddy might be perfect for you!

CHAPTER 3

CHOOSING A PUPPY

Your research is clear and the verdict for the best possible puppy for your family is a Teddy Bear. Congratulations! Now you can just go out and make a purchase, right? WRONG! Your journey to find the best dog is just beginning. Choosing the right breed (or hybrid) is a great first step. But buying a dog is a big commitment - a commitment for life. So the process of selecting the right breed attributes for your lifestyle is critical. Careful consideration and choosing the right puppy can offer a quality life of unconditional love and companionship, good temperament, and health. Making a haphazard decision can mean 10 or more years of spiraling medical bills, devastating illness, ending in heartbreak at death.

Where to Locate Your Puppy

The Teddy Bear is not a purebred dog but a hybrid of two or three different breeds. Typically a breeder will cross a purebred Bichon Frisé with a Shih Tzu (making a Shichon or Zuchon), or they will mate a Bichon Frisé with a toy Poodle (making a Poochon) creating an F1 "designer dog." They may combine a purebred dam or sire with a hybrid mate, creating an F1b offspring, or breed two F1 mates creating a F2 offspring. Two F2 mates will produce F3 offspring. Beyond that the cross is considered a "multigenerational hybrid," and we will need to consult a calculator to evaluate all the factors involved. In addition to the Bichon Frisé, Shih Tzu and toy Poodle, purebred dogs used in the creation of Teddy Bear puppies include Yorkshire Terriers and minia-ture Schnauzers.

Since the Teddy Bear is a mixed breed, it is not a part of the American Kennel Club or any purebred registry. There is no pedigree to track in an effort to determine genetic dispositions. The popularity, consumer demand, and cost of the enchanting Teddy Bear dogs inspire human greed in full force, so while finding a good, responsible breeder may be tricky, the search is essential.

If you are looking for a quality Teddy Bear puppy, you should start with the sanctioned clubs representing one of the purebred parents in the mix:

- The Bichon Frisé Club of America
- The Poodle Club of America
- The American Shih Tzu Club

Breeders of the purebred dogs may participate in the mating of the hybrids or know of a good Teddy Bear breeder to recommend. Other viable search options include the American Kennel Club (AKC), which maintains a database of breed organizations and breeder listings for possible contacts. An organization identified as the International Designer Canine Registry (IDCR) provides a breeder list for the various popular design-er breeds and allows a certificate source for hybrid dogs. The American Canine Hybrid Club (ACHC) also does this. Participation or recognition in any breeder club or orga-nization does not guarantee that a breeder is responsible or that they produce quality dogs. It is but one more step in your discovery.

Your local veterinarian or groomer may have contact information for credible breed-ers known for producing healthy, happy puppies. Selecting a great breeder is critical to ensure the future health and well-being of a dog. DO NOT buy a dog from a pet store! Nearly every dog sold in a retail environment is the product of a commercial breeding facility (puppy mill). Do your homework. Commit the time and effort to finding a re-sponsible breeder whose concern is healthy, quality dogs before you buy.

Back to Basics - How to Spot the Best Breeder

Adding a perfect Teddy Bear pup to your family should not be the result of an impulse buy. It is a commitment that demands patience, research, investigation, and due diligence.

Once you locate a breeder of interest, the interview should begin. The Humane Society of the US provides a downloadable list of important questions to ask. As a prospective buyer, do not be reluctant to ask for a consultation and references (be sure to check them). A good breeder will not be offended; in fact, they should be happy to talk about their dogs. If a breeder is unwilling to be interviewed, is short in her responses, does not seem knowledgeable about the breed, or is pushy for the sale, walk away.

Plan to visit the kennel where the puppies are being nurtured. A good breeder will NOT sell a dog to someone they haven't met in person. You should feel encouraged to spend time with the puppies and interact with the litter. Make multiple visits if desired. Watch for red flags such as:

• The mother of the litter is not on the premises

• Dogs are kept in cramped, dirty kennels

• Several dogs of various breeds are on the grounds

• Multiple litters are enclosed with several nursing females

• There are multiple pregnant females

• Dogs are restrained on chains

• Multiple dogs are held together in pens

• Dogs on the premise are dirty or appear malnourished or sick

• Females deliver a litter every 6 months

Do not fall for the clean, cute corral of puppies inside a house or garage with no other visible dogs on the premise. Brokers will often purchase a litter from a commercial facility and sell to unsuspecting buyers as "home-bred dogs." Make sure you see the parents - at the very least the mother and the whelping facility.

Any good breeder cares deeply about their breeding program, but more importantly, they care about the dogs they produce. They will encourage visits to their kennel and invite the entire family. As a prospective buyer you should expect to complete a purchase application and provide references. They will be interested in why you will make a good pet parent for one of their precious puppies. Expect to answer questions such as:

• Why do you want a Teddy Bear puppy?

• How much time will you have for the care of the puppy?

• Do you have other pets?

• Do you have small children?

• Do you have a fenced yard?

• Can you provide adequate exercise, mental stimulation, and so cialization for your puppy?

• What are your training plans?

• Are you prepared to provide adequate grooming?

Do not be alarmed if the breeder does not choose to sell a puppy to you immediately. In fact, many breeders will hold off on making a decision and will even put prospective buyers on a "wait list." They do not sell to the first person with cash in hand. They want to find the right home for their dog and the decision could come down to a gut instinct. It may take a certain commitment from a buyer to exhibit persistence to make the connection stick.

Get What You Pay For - Contracts and Guarantees

The price of your Teddy Bear should be relative to the amount of testing and care given to the breeding process. It is not a cheap proposition, and most breeders do not realize a break even on their investment. Passionate breeders breed for the love of their dogs, NOT JUST FOR PROFIT.

A responsible breeder will require a sales contract. Contract language will include a spay/neuter agreement and the commitment that the dog must be returned to their care should the adoption not work out at any time or for any reason.

A quality breeder will provide a packet of information in addition to health and pedigree including: grooming instructions, nutrition and diet details, breed-specific information, and exercise and training recommendations. They will provide ongoing support as you raise your puppy. The "thirty-day, money back guarantee" is not an option for a good breeder; they consider their dogs' welfare for LIFE.

The Puppies' Parents

To create a perfect Teddy Bear puppy, the following must be considered:

- Excellent health and great temperaments for both dam and sire
- Hip, elbow, and joint evaluations
- Eyes, teeth, and jaw confirmation
- Extensive blood tests to determine genetic markers for epilepsy and other disorders

- The mating dogs should be a minimum of two years of age before their first litter of puppies

- A female dog should have at least a year to recover before she is allowed to become pregnant again

Teddy Bears do not have the advantage of a generational pedigree, but the parents of the breeding program should. Check for any genetic issues in the line(s). Confirmation of health tests from a licensed veterinarian for both parents and any generational information should be expected.

Health Tests and Certificates

When a dam becomes pregnant, she should enter a comprehensive prenatal program. Good nutrition, exercise, and medical care are critical to prevent congenital issues. Most breeders will request an ultrasound evaluation of the uterus to determine the number of puppies and to identify any potential issues with the delivery. Additional health tests of both the mother and her offspring are an indicator of good health. You should expect certificates of health including worming and inoculations at regular intervals from birth by a qualified veterinarian when you purchase your dog.

I Pick You! - Choosing One Puppy from the Litter

Great breeders have taken the subjectivity of choice from the prospective buyer. This is especially true of popular, in-demand puppies like Teddy Bears. An informed breeder will consider the role the puppy is supposed to play in the family from information provided in the purchase application. Behavior and health tests are significant indicators of temperament and behavior. A family with small children and other pets may not be able to handle the personality of an alpha male; similarly, a family interested in entering their Teddy Bear in a special companion program may need the confidence and spirit of the alpha. The burden of choice is often moved from the hands of the potential buyer and the decision is made by the breeder. But how is the personality determined in an infant dog?

Testing a puppy's personality to determine their future capabilities as an adult began as an extension of testing children's learning abilities in the 1950s. In the 1960s, tests were stylized to include a determinant of the potential for a canine's dominance or submission. These tests were further improved and today the battery is considered a leading indicator of a dog's behavioral traits as adults. Known as the Volhard Puppy Aptitude Test, the system is used broadly by breeders, trainers, and handlers in determining a dog's "right home." There are no losers in the test-only WINNERS when there is the proper match.

Beyond the technology of testing, there are determinants to consider when visiting a kennel with a litter of cute, lovable, excited puppies.

- A puppy will exhibit his/her best potential at 8-10 weeks of age. A good breeder would NOT let a puppy leave the litter before 8 weeks.

- Consider taking a trainer, groomer, veterinarian, or vet tech with you when you visit the kennel to help with the selection process.

- Look for the happy, active, playful pup.

- Pick the puppy up - it should be round and wriggly, not fat, and certainly not skinny. Even inherently thin breeds like Greyhounds are pudgy puppies.

- Look for the pup that struts his stuff: the confident personality with a high head and a wiggly tail - consider an excited slurp of a kiss a bonus.

- Look for bright eyes and a clean, shiny coat, clear ears, and no debris or discharge from tip to tail (especially tail!).

- Be wary of an anxious, fearful, shy pup. A puppy at 8-10 weeks of age should not show these traits.

- Conduct a hearing test. With the puppy facing away from you, stamp your foot, whistle, or drop keys. Make sure the pup reacts to the noise by turning, jumping, or expressing curiosity.

- Pick the puppy up and turn him/her on their back. They should calm and allow you to stroke their belly. If the dog objects and fails to settle it is a bad sign.

- You should be able to touch the puppy all over: mouth, ears, nose, feet, toes, tummy, and tail without objection.

- Make sure the litter has been screened for genetic conditions.

- The breeder should allow your personal veterinarian screening upon purchase with a money-back guarantee if health defects are discovered.

Adopt Before You Shop

The Humane Society reports that more than 2.7 million pets are euthanized each year in the United States. Consider adopting from a rescue shelter before you shop. Adoption from shelters assures a healthy pet. Most shelters fully vet, vaccinate, spay/neuter, and evaluate temperament and behavior prior to placing an animal on the available list.

Adopting a rescue dog is considerably less expensive than buying a puppy. An adult rescue dog spares the puppy phases that many pet owners find most difficult. Adopting an adult dog is a what-you-see-is-what-you-get proposition. But even with pricey hybrids there is the element of the unknown - which breed will my puppy most represent? By adopting from a shelter, the unknown is removed!

What about rescuing a senior dog? The American Society for the Prevention of Cruelty to Animals (ASPCA) provides a compelling list for people interested in adopting a senior dog. Consider the following:

• What you see is what you get. No surprises here; the senior dog is full grown: color, confirmation, temperament, andeverything in between is laid out for inspection and acceptance.

• Low demands: senior dogs are just easier. They will be happy to lay at your feet and listen to the television or snore while you read a book.

- Limited drama: senior dogs do not require the monitoring, training, and patience that puppies do. Basically, they are just happy hanging with the family.

- Training is complete: there's no puppy frenzy, a time which drives many new dog owners to the brink.

- Couch potato friendly: senior dogs will happily nap all day. They will require the occasional potty walk but not the revolving door of a puppy.

Yes, Teddy Bear dogs are available for adoption. Check Pet Finder, the national database for rescue and shelter animals, for more information about Teddy Bears in search of forever homes!

Finding the Perfect Puppy

You want a perfect puppy? Stop looking now. Puppies, like people, are never perfect. To imagine a living being capable of fulfilling your every expectation is simply not realistic. Puppies poop and pee in inappropriate places. They bark and whine and have other distracting, irritating habits. They chew expensive shoes and soil heirloom rugs. They will eat nearly anything. Many a chair, table, or bed has been reduced to splinters by the teething, boredom, or insatiable curiosity of a puppy. They run, jump, dash and dive. During the fateful, hours of the night, they become sonic projectiles.

Owning a puppy means tolerating late night howling and crying and learning to function with serious sleep deprivation. Puppies issue ear-splitting objections to being confined to a crate. They require frequent cleaning up as a result of missed puppy pads and they vomit gross, undigested objects at your feet. They roll in disgusting, foul-smelling gunk with glee and subsequently need frequent baths. Puppies are not easy, they are not convenient, and they are not subject to short cuts. They require patience, training, persistence, tolerance, and much love.

What they deliver is the comical, whimsical, full-tilt frenzy and infectious happiness that only a puppy brings. They snuggle, kiss, and simply adore you despite your most offensive human actions. No one can experience a totally bad day with a puppy. Puppies grow into dogs that with just a little nurturing and guidance provide unconditional love and complete devotion. They ask so little and return so much.

So to find the perfect Teddy Bear puppy, or any other dog, you simply need to commit to working on becoming the perfect pet owner. If you fall short, no worries; your dog will most definitely forgive you and love you just the same!

CHAPTER 4

PUPPY-PROOFING YOUR HOUSE

B ringing home a Teddy Bear puppy is an exciting day for your family! Making your home a safe environment is essential to the health and welfare of your new puppy.

Teddy Bears are small dogs and they will require an extra measure of protection. An adult Teddy Bear may weigh 10 to 12 pounds, but a puppy could weigh only a pound or two when you adopt. Don't let the tiny package fool you; they are also full of energy and curiosity. A fearless nature and unbridled desire to check out anything of remote interest can lead your Teddy Bear into dangerous situations. The typical house is full of hazards for puppies, so pet-proofing is necessary to protect your new family member. Exercising a few precautions can ensure a peaceful home.

Introducing a Teddy Bear to Resident Pets

Part of the Pack

The excitement of bringing home a new puppy is not always contagious. Do not expect every family member to welcome the new addition with open hands - or paws. Other pets may not feel the love for the trespasser in their family. Puppies are rude, they bite, and they will not sit still for the proper "sniff test," so older animals are immediately put on guard. The cute, furry youngsters that are so adorable to the human members of the pack might look very different to other pets, especially resident dogs and cats. They see competition - a nuisance at best - and they may even view the newcomer as a potential snack. Be patient and exercise a few basic precautions to ease the pack integration process.

Stage a neutral area for the puppy. Do not put the newcomer near the established common areas of other dogs or cats. Try to keep existing feeding, sleeping, and litter box areas as undisturbed as possible. If you need to rearrange housing for your other pets, make changes before the new arrival so the older pets do not associate the disruption of their domain with the puppy.

Do not scold or punish the animals if they do not get along at first. You can't force family members to like one another.

Keep the puppy in a crate or confined area away from existing pets. If a resident pet expresses interest, encourage interaction.

First is first: condition yourself to acknowledge the existing animals first, play with them first, and give them treats first.

Feed resident pets at the same time(s) you feed the puppy. Always separate the feeding areas to avoid possible food aggression.

Do not ignore the resident dog in favor of the puppy. If the older pet approaches for attention stop playing with the puppy and reassure the existing pet. Puppies do demand attention, but it's important not to let your new dog push the others aside for your favor.

Schedule supervised play times after meals. Full bellies will calm, tire, and provide for a more relaxed social atmosphere.

When mild altercations arise, do not step in. Let the animals develop their own pecking order in the pack. Some drama may occur, accompanied by growling and snarling, but unless you fear a true physical threat, stay calm and let them work it out. If you are concerned about physical danger, muzzle the older dogs until you are sure everyone can play safe.

Bring in a professional if the transition between the resident pet(s) and the new puppy just isn't working.

Circle of Safety

It is difficult to imagine, but inside the house could very well be the most dangerous place in your Teddy Bear puppy's world. Pets do not understand the hazards to avoid in the human household. It is hard - maybe even impossible - to anticipate everything your dog may get into. A good look around each room, the garage, and the yard for the most common hazards will give the circle of safety a good start.

Kitchen and Dining Area

Dogs will eat just about anything. The kitchen and dining area will be a smorgasbord of interesting smells and tastes. Puppies learn quickly that the kitchen is where the good stuff is located. Common kitchen items that can cause a great deal of trouble include the following:

- Cleaning materials - sponges, caustic detergents, mothballs, furniture polish, dishwasher pods
- Human foods - alcohol, avocados, chocolate, coffee, grapes, any product (especially chewing gum) with xylitol
- Food bones
- Food trays and wrappers
- Plastic bags (especially used browning bags)
- Rodent bait and insecticides
- Electric cords
- Batteries
- Coins

The trash can offers a puppy the most allure and also poses the biggest danger. Make sure the trash is stored in a metal container that cannot be tipped over. A lid should cover the opening. Never leave a bag of waste exposed where the dog can tear into the contents.

An ambitious puppy will work tirelessly to get at the object of desire. Install cabinet safety locks to prevent doors from easily opening and exposing dangerous contents.

Check for electric cords, open doors through which your puppy can see stairs, and exits offering opportunities to escape.

Install baby gates at door openings leading to non-secure, off-limits areas.

The dining room may seem like a safe place for the pooch but be aware of potential risks there as well.

• Candles and liquid potpourri

• Plants and flowers used in arrangements

• Exposed electric outlets

Consider securing your Teddy Bear in a confined space during dinnertime, especially with guests. Teddy Bears are small and may accidentally be stepped on. A guest with little knowledge may also be tempted to feed your pup human food. Having a puppy around humans eating does not enforce good training practices. Better safe than sorry!

Danger in the Bathroom and Laundry

The bathroom and laundry room appear to be wonderful options for confining a curious puppy. They are convenient spaces to secure an animal and they can remain in a safe room, unsupervised for hours. GREAT idea! Just check and double-check for potential dangers such as:

• Exposed electric cords

• Open drains

• Soap and detergents

• Loose laundry (dogs can choke on small articles of clothing and chewed buttons)

• Coins and buttons

• Open trash cans

• Bath salts

• Toilet bowl cleaners

Make sure the toilet lid remains closed to prevent the risk of drowning and front-loading dryer doors are closed. Cabinets should have security locks installed.

Beware of the Garage

The garage is another room that holds treasures of fascination for a puppy. Items to check and remove to prevent accidental poisoning or injury to your dog include:

• Antifreeze

• Paint

• Detergents and cleaners

• Screws, pins, and nails

• Motor oil

• Gasoline

• Windshield washer fluid

• Turpentine

• Battery acid

• Insecticides and pesticides

• Saws, blades, knives, and other tools

Remember to check for exposed fluids in containers as well as any that may have leaked from a vehicle.

A dog locked in the garage, intentionally or by accident, will bolt when the door opens. Enter and exit the garage with care to avoid hitting your precious pup with a vehicle or pinning him under the closing automatic garage door.

Outside Fences and Yards

A fenced yard can be a puppy's dream and an owner's nightmare. Appropriate fencing should be installed for the size and type of dog. A Teddy Bear pup does not require a 6 feet tall, chain-link enclosure for confinement. In fact, some of the decorative fences designed for large dogs would not be safe for your puppy. A small dog can slither through pickets and slats and get caught in chain links. They can slide under fence gaps between the ground and the fencing borders.

Based on the size and athletic ability of your Teddy Bear, he may be able to leap over a three-foot-tall enclosure. Check the fence perimeter frequently to ensure that there are no newly excavated escape holes. Gates that do not close properly are also a problem, and if you have a little escape artist, look out - they will break out. Remember that in addition to keeping your Teddy bear IN, you are keeping other animals OUT.

Decorative flowers and shrubs may pose a health risk for your dog(s). Lovely plants like the following are dangerous for your dog:

• Amaryllis	• Elephant ears	• Lily of the Valley
• Crocus	• Gladiolas	• Tulip
• Daffodil	• Hyacinth	

These flowers are a curiosity. Your curious dog might be tempted to eat the blooms, which are toxic.

The list is far from complete, but it represents some of the most common ornamental landscaping plants. Any of them can make your Teddy Bear dog sick, so be sure to evaluate your yard for a pet-friendly environment. A comprehensive list of non-toxic and poisonous plants, hazardous solvents, and other household dangers is provided by the ASPCA.

Holiday Tips

Holidays bring their own brand of dangers for pets.

Halloween candy may be dropped in unusual places for your Teddy Bear's discovery. Watch your dog on walks to make sure he doesn't find his own brand of "treat." Trick-or-treaters scare many dogs. Keep your dog in her "safe room" during trick-or-treat hours. Play a radio or television so they won't be disturbed by the frequently ringing doorbell. Remember that:

- Chocolate in all forms, especially dark chocolate, can be fatal for dogs (and cats).

- Candies and gum containing Xylitol and other artificial sweeteners are dangerous for pets.

- Candy wrappers, foil, and cellophane, when ingested, can cause intestinal blockages, vomiting, or diarrhea

Thanksgiving is a holiday when many people and pets travel to spend time with family and friends. Make sure you are satisfied with the pet-proofing of any guest quarters.

Christmas trees inside the house, pretty packages, ornaments, candles, food, candy, fires, and a little sip of bubbly! 'Tis the season for pet-proofing the festive decorations!

- Certain plants like poinsettias and holly are toxic if ingested
- Tinsel, gift ribbons, and ornaments pose a choking hazard for dogs
- Fireplaces and candles can burn your dog, and candle wax causes digestive problems if swallowed
- Alcohol in candy, baked goods, or by itself is toxic for dogs

New Year's Eve and **Fourth of July** celebrations often feature loud, bright, bursting booms of fireworks. They scare many dogs to the point of future phobic behavior. Make sure you crate or otherwise secure your dog during such festivities. Never force him into an environment that creates stress and fear.

Learn and practice first aid procedures with your family - including those family members with four legs. Post emergency contact numbers in an easy-to-locate place. Include your human emergency responders as well as the Animal Poison Control Hot Line. Establishing a safer environment for your pets may cost a bit of time, but the peace of mind you receive in return is priceless!

CHAPTER 5

THE FIRST FEW DAYS

Having a Plan

The first day you bring home your new teddy bear pup, everyone will be excited. You'll be excited. Your family will be excited. The puppy will be excited. You will have a blast introducing your little fuzzball to his new home. But what comes next? It is important to have a specific plan to help your puppy smoothly assimilate into life in your home. This involves making a strategy in advance with your family: puppy-proofing the house, being prepared with supplies, and hitting the ground running with training. Young pups of all breeds are always a challenge, and the Teddy Bear is no different, but the joy they bring to the house is more than worth the work. Take some time before the dog arrives to plan out exactly how you want things to go. With preparation, your first days with your puppy will be much easier.

Preparing the Kids

Not every household has children, but if you have kids, especially little ones, they need to understand exactly how to treat a new puppy. Remember, Teddy Bears are very tiny at 8 weeks old, when many new owners take them home. At this age, they weigh less than two pounds and, while they're sturdy little pups, children need to know to be gentle. Just because the puppy looks like a teddy bear doesn't mean it can be treated like one.

Kids will be very excited on the day you pick up your puppy, so sit them down days in advance. Explain that this puppy is just a baby. It is just learning about the world and it needs to know that you are his trusted friend. Puppies shouldn't have their tails pulled or get squeezed hard like teddy bears. They also shouldn't be chased if they are feeling scared or tired. New puppies can tire out quickly (don't worry, Teddies get almost unlimited energy with time) and need quiet time to sleep. This can be a good time for children to cuddle the puppy, making it feel warm and secure with your kids.

Kids should also have a hand in feeding, training, and cleaning up after the pup. When playing, kids shouldn't push the puppy to "play bite" or behave badly. Also, new puppies need a schedule to help with their learning. Children can learn to feed them in the morning and take them out at specific times for potty training. Kids at different ages can handle different dog jobs, so let them help out with whatever you think is best. Use these teachable moments to help alleviate your load of responsibilities and give your kids a feeling of true dog ownership. By learning how to care for their new Teddy Bear puppy, they'll learn responsibility and strengthen the "best friend bond" with their dog that will last for many years to come.

The Ride Home

This is a big moment for a baby Teddy! She is leaving the place where she was born, her mom, and her littermates, and she's getting in a big metal box and driving away with you! Good news: most teddy bear pups love the journey. But it's also important to be prepared and give them a safe, welcoming environment. This is the best method I know, and it has worked like a charm for me and my dogs.

❶ Feed and water the puppy. They shouldn't eat or drink too much; just enough to make sure they're not hungry or thirsty on the road. If they are too full, they are more likely to get carsick or have an accident.

❷ Make sure they have pooped and peed before you get on the road.

❸ Run them around a little bit. A happy and tired Teddy is the perfect candidate for a first car ride.

❹ Have a couple of thick towels laid out on the passenger side seat of your vehicle. If your teddy is fairly calm, this will be their spot.

❺ Have a human co-pilot to ride along in the back seat. That way they can help wrangle a wiggly puppy so you can keep your attention on the road.

❻ Have a small crate set up in the back seat or trunk, just in case the pup isn't doing well in the front seat. You can always pull over and have her settle down.

❼ Always be calm and encouraging. If possible, don't give your pup any attention while you drive. She should learn that this is not the time to play with her people.

❽ Take your time. This isn't the time to set a new land speed record. If you need to pull over and help your teddy, do it.

Best-case scenario, your Teddy will sit quietly in the passenger seat, maybe sleep, and enjoy the ride. When you first start the engine, they may be surprised. Just stay calm and they will learn that there is nothing to fear. Once you're on the road, gently try to keep them in their seat. If they try to climb onto your lap, just nudge them back into place, without making eye contact or saying a word. This will help them learn that the passenger seat is their spot when they are riding. If necessary, crack the windows and turn on the AC so they feel comfortable. If they won't sit still or feel insecure, have another blanket set up in the wheel well in front of their seat. Moving them to the floor may do the trick. You can always put them in the backseat crate if this doesn't work.

With all this preparation, your first car ride will probably go smoothly. Teddy Bear puppies are excited to be with you, experiencing new things. But it never hurts to be prepared. By setting the tone on this first car ride and making sure your puppy is happy, they will grow up into a fantastic car companion.

The First Night

I will recommend crate training over and over in this book, and this is the method I explain here. Some people want to let the new pup sleep in bed with them. This may be what some owners want, but be careful; you'll have a bed companion for life, and you'll also risk nighttime accidents on your clean sheets. I recommend putting your Teddy in a small dog crate in your bedroom or just outside the door. Because your puppy has never been away from the warm bodies of their mom and littermates before, he will probably cry, whimper, whine, and howl alone in his crate at night. They may keep it up for most of the night! Plan for this, and let it pass. With time, he'll get used to the situation, becoming very secure in his new crate.

Take your Teddy out to potty right before bed. He'll probably go bit by bit for a few minutes before he's completely done. When he looks like he has done all he's going to do, pick him up and praise him so he knows he did well. Then carry him to his crate and put him down for bed. The area in his crate should just be big enough for him to lie down. Puppies usually won't soil their bed area, because they know it's their den. Once inside, they should be accident-free for the evening. Pet him and encourage him, then latch the door and go to bed. This is usually when the whimpering starts. Just let him go, though it can be heartbreaking to listen to him. If he keeps it up for a long time, it can be appropriate to go to him, gently pick him up by the scruff of the neck, and say, "Go to sleep." Just don't go to him too often when he cries. He'll learn that this is a good way to get you to do what he wants.

After a few days left alone in his crate at night, your Teddy Bear will start to sleep more quietly. Eventually he won't whimper at all. By crate training at night, you'll curtail or eliminate nighttime accidents and set a standard for good bedtime behavior. Just stick with it! Bedtime crying can be exhausting, but you know it's coming, so decide now how you're going to work with your puppy. With compassionate and consistent care, your little guy will be sleeping through the night in no time.

First Vet Visit

Your new teddy will need a series of immunizations before being exposed to other dogs and public places like dog parks. This will require taking your pup to the vet a few times during her first months with you. Follow the instructions above for the car ride to the

vet. Have some training treats in your pocket so she will have positive associations with the vet's office. Also bring along her favorite chew toy for her to gnaw on when you get to the vet. She can chew away at this in the waiting room and again when you get into the exam room. By giving her an activity to keep her preoccupied, she will have a distraction from the anxiety that vet visits can bring. Your vet will know how to make your pup comfortable even when she has to get shots. Just take your time and give her lots of encouragement. Your pup should do really well, even at her very first vet visit.

Do Teddy Bears Need School?

Training programs are a great choice for any dog, even tiny ones like Teddy Bears. Even though Teddies are very small, they are very smart and enjoy a challenge. Obedience school can be an excellent companion to training at home. It has lots of benefits.

For one thing, your teddy will get much-needed socialization at training classes. She'll be around new people and unfamiliar dogs in a brand-new setting. Puppies need to learn that new doesn't mean threatening. Some puppies seem to know this naturally, but others need to be socialized by having numerous positive experiences with new people and animals. Training classes give them plenty of these experiences in a safe, structured learning environment.

At training school, your Teddy will also learn important manners and commands. It is vital that every dog knows basic commands like "sit," "stay," and "come" very dependably. If your dog ever ends up outside off-leash in an unsafe place, you need to be sure that he will listen to you so you can leash him before he gets hurt or lost. A training class is a focused opportunity to have professional help with these basic commands. Your teddy bear needs a firm foundation for behavior during his first few months with you. If he learns how to behave early, he will be a much better pet for the rest of his life.

If obedience school is not an option, take time every day to work with your puppy on at least basic commands. Reward him often with little training treats (these are available at most pet stores). Also arrange safe interactions with new people and animals, as long as his immunizations are up-to-date. When your puppy learns to trust that new people are a good thing, he'll be a great friend to everyone. With obedience training at home and in class, he'll know exactly how to behave when he meets these new friends.

Necessary Supplies

First of all, puppy-proof your house before you bring your dog home for the first time. A new puppy should not have free reign over an entire house, and she should never be out of your sight, unless she is in her crate. Section off a puppy-safe area in your home, with an easy-to-clean floor, where the dog can romp and play without getting into trouble. This area should be free of dangling power cords, chemicals, houseplants, string, small objects, nooks and crannies to get lost in, and anything you don't want chewed. For the first week or so, your puppy should always be here, in her crate, or closely monitored in other safe places around your home.

You should also have these items ready when your Teddy Bear comes home for the first time:

- **A small crate, bed, and carrier.** A crate should have enough space for her to lay down comfortably. These are available with built-in expanders, to grow with your dog. A puppy should also have a small bed or two so she always knows where in your home it is appropriate for her to sleep. A carrier is very handy if you need to take her somewhere and don't want her running loose.

- **Good quality, dry, small-breed puppy food.** Puppies have different metabolic needs than adult dogs, so kibble formulated especially for small-breed puppies is a must. You should have some canned, wet food available too, to mix in with the hard stuff and provide added flavor and hydration.

- **Puppy-safe toys, chews, and treats.** Don't get cheap plush toys that can be easily ripped open (though excellent plush toys are available). Buy durable toys that can't be swallowed or damaged by new puppy teeth. Your teething puppy will need a lot to chew, so provide him with chews that will last a long time and won't give him an upset stomach. Training treats are a great way to reinforce good behavior in these first days at home.

- **Potty pads for inside the house.** These sometimes work well for little dogs. If your puppy has to go all of a sudden, she can learn that the pad is her emergency spot. Or, if you live high up in an apartment complex or can't make it outside quickly for some reason, potty pads can get a great permanent spot for your puppy to do her business. Think of it like a puppy litter box. Potty pads are highly absorbent, perfect for this purpose.

- **Water and food bowls.** Have bowls dedicated just for your Teddy Bear. Make sure they can't be knocked over by a clumsy puppy and aren't too big. You don't want your puppy falling into her water bowl!

- **Collar, ID, and leash.** Your Teddy pup should always wear a well-fitting collar and ID tag with her name, your name, your address, and your phone number. A retractable leash is a great option for small dogs like this, but you can choose any one you like, so long as it isn't too heavy for a tiny puppy.

- **Waste bags.** These are necessities. I buy these by the case. I opt for biodegradable rolls, each with 20 bags. I always keep a fresh roll hanging on my dog's leash.

- **Grooming products.** Your new puppy will need regular brushing to avoid mats in her long hair. A brush with thick, ball-tipped bristles works especially well for fur like this. Also be prepared with puppy-friendly shampoo, nail clippers, and flea/tick treatment for puppies (check that out with your vet). Your puppy probably won't like brushing and nail trimming at first, but stick with it; she'll get used to it.

Cost Breakdown for the First Year

Puppies aren't the most expensive addition you could make to your life, but they certainly aren't the cheapest. Teddy Bear pups may have some needs that you don't anticipate, so here is a breakdown of what you'll spend during your first year with your dog.

- **Food -** $50-$100 or more. This depends, of course, on the kind of food you buy. Lucky for you, Teddy Bears are tiny and don't eat very much. This being the case, take the opportunity to spend the extra cash on some healthy food for your growing buddy.

- **Medical -** $200-$300. Vet bills vary a lot, depending on the practice and location. Most of this cost is early checkups and immunizations. Once your pup is up-to-date with her early life vet care needs, this cost will be lower. It doesn't hurt to have some money set aside for emergencies, but most teddy bears don't have big problems as pups.

- **Toys and treats -** $50. Budget higher if you plan on spoiling your little guy.

- **License -** $15-$25. The cost depends on your location. It's important to get your pup legal. Have him registered soon after you get him.

- **Spay or neuter -** $50-$200. Spays cost a lot more than neuters, and the cost of both varies depending on where they are performed. You'll have a couple of months to figure out where to get your pup spayed or neutered. Your trusted vet is a great choice, but clinics for lower cost operations are also sometimes available.

- **Collar, leash, crate, and bed -** $50-$200. I have gotten reliable crate hand-me-downs from friends, but I like to buy beds new. This all depends on where you shop. Always buy quality, but it is not necessary to break the bank.

- **Grooming** - $50-$200. This can be done at home for free, or you can get your Teddy the royal treatment at a salon. Teddy Bears can look very fancy with the right do, but only you can know if that's the way you want to go. They also look adorable in full-on shaggy gremlin mode.

- **Miscellaneous other costs** - $100-$200. This can be anything: additional vet bills, training classes, special automatic treat dispenser.... Puppies tend to be doted upon, so know in advance that you'll probably want to treat your Teddy every now and then.

Teddy Bear puppies are a joyous addition to any household, but they bring with them certain challenges. By making a detailed plan in advance, everyone will be happier during these first few days. Your puppy will be set up for success, and you won't have any major surprises. Have patience. By raising a Teddy Bear puppy right, you'll have a loving and devoted pal for many years to come.

CHAPTER 6

THE FIRST WEEKS WITH YOUR TEDDY BEAR PUPPY

Fragile!

You hold that sweet bundle of fur and immediately fall hopelessly in love with your Teddy Bear puppy. Chances are the little darling will be able to fit in the palm of your hand, and you'll worry about breaking him. Don't stress too much. Teddy Bears are strong, hardy dogs; however, extra care is warranted. In addition to puppy-proofing your house, there are some important precautions you can take for this tiny one's protection.

Small and toy breeds have special needs that are not considerations for larger dogs. By merit of size they are prone to injury by other pets and people - especially children. You can't be everywhere or anticipate every move your new charge will make. Trying to overprotect will make you both crazy. The best use of your concern is to ensure a safe environment and immediately begin training for the little dog and his new family.

The most common injuries to puppies and small or toy dogs are the result of:

• Jumping off furniture

• Leaping out of a human's arms

• Getting stepped on

• Rough play with other dogs and children.

Teddy Bear puppies tend to be daring, adventurous, and very, very curious. His energy is off the chain and he doesn't understand his physical limitations. A dog's bones are forming for up to the first year of life, so it is a fragile time. You will want to exercise caution when playing with your puppy during the critical, formative first year.

Do not encourage jumping from sofas, chairs, beds or other relatively high objects. Consider installing puppy steps and teach your Teddy Bear to use them if she is allowed on the furniture.

Work with your Teddy Bear and her human playmates slowly. It is best to keep the dog leashed while the pup and a child are getting acquainted. Teddy Bear puppies are especially delightful because of their resemblance to a child's toy bear. Make sure the child understands the puppy is NOT a toy and it must be handled with care and respect.

Before the first meeting explain the nature of a puppy to the child. Emphasize the tendency to bite, jump and scratch. Explain that the dog doesn't mean to hurt and doesn't understand, but it is NOT appropriate behavior. Instruct the child about the appropriate way to discipline the dog when he or she misbehaves. NEVER let a child think hitting, kicking, biting, or hurting the dog in any way is ever okay.

Teach the child the correct method to hold a Teddy Bear and explain the fragile nature of their small bodies and tender bones. Your puppy will become a better-adjusted dog with frequent exposure to children. Never leave a puppy unsupervised with a small child.

It is advisable to keep your young Teddy Bear secluded from other dogs until his vaccinations are up to date. Supervise introductions with your other pets. Approach strange dogs with caution and keep your puppy within reach if you feel the need to intervene. Make sure the newcomer is properly leashed and under the owner's control at all times.

If you are in a crowded place with your Teddy Bear, keep her in your arms or use stroller or puppy carrier for transportation and to avoid having an unsuspecting pedestrian step on the small dog.

The first few weeks of settling with your new puppy will establish the tone for life. Keep in mind her small body and special requirements but don't coddle. With a healthy dose of caution, you can make your Teddy Bear's transition to her new world one that leaves her well-adjusted, confident, and healthy.

Setting Firm Boundaries

Teddy Bear dogs have the reputation of being affectionate, smart, friendly, and easy to train. Like all pets, a well-behaved, sweet natured Teddy Bear is a pleasure to own and a delight to be around. Unfortunately, a puppy that is not brought up well has the tendency to become snarly, yippy, ill-natured, wary, suspicious, unpleasant to encounter, and a headache to live with. Genetics and health aside, the kind of dog you have depends a great deal on YOU and the foundation you establish from the very first day.

You leave the kennel with a sweet, cuddly, happy puppy. If you are lucky you will get home before the heart-wrenching crying, howling, barking, scratching, and other overall objections to your puppy's new home begin. You must remember that this journey is most likely the first time your puppy has been away from her mother and litter mates. The pup is scared and lonely; she wants comfort. It is easy to pick her up and tuck her in bed with you. But unless sleeping in your bed is one of the habits you plan to carry on-for life-don't do it! It is essential for you to set firm boundaries from the first day. Firm boundaries not just for your puppy, but for you too!

By adopting a puppy you have assumed the job of mother. Your puppy will look to you for examples, lessons, and discipline in order to learn the behaviors he will carry into adulthood. You will establish where and when he eats and sleeps. You will determine the appropriate place and time to go potty, when and how to play with others. From this point forward your dog will be conditioned by your control.

Establish a schedule. Stick to your routine. Fortunately, there are tools to help. Perhaps the most effective (and most difficult) is the crate. Successful crate training is often a test of will.

Canine experts generally agree about the advantages of crate training a puppy. It is one of the more difficult housing adjustments, but the practical applications are many. It is hard for most owners to close their precious pup in a locked container. The howls that the puppy lets out during the first few sessions will be painful to endure. Many people abandon crate training in favor of a good night's sleep. Puppies typically behave like they are in the chamber of torment but if you can hold firm and jump the hurdle of the first two or three restless nights, both you and your dog will benefit.

A crate provides a safe haven for your dog. Puppies eventually view the crate as their special den (dogs are den animals, after all). Once the dog adjusts, a crate becomes a powerful stepping stone for a good many other training elements as discussed in later chapters. Reassure yourself you have provided a comfortable nest for your puppy. Choose the right container for your dog's size and breed. You may start with a small crate for a puppy and graduate to a larger container.

- The container should be large enough for the dog to stand, stretch, and lay down comfortably.

- Place the crate in an area where the puppy will see activity. Puppies are comforted when they are with their people.

- Place the crate in the bedroom; the puppy will recognize sleep patterns and learn to settle for the night.

- Place a highly desired treat in the crate as a reward. He will know that is the best place to find his favorite treat.

- Never remove a fussy puppy from the crate. Wait until he is calm.

- Never use confinement in the crate as punishment.

Training tools are important, but the most effective method of training your dog is your communication. Dogs learn by reinforcement. If the result of the behavior is that the puppy gets what he wants, he will keep doing it regardless of whether it's right or wrong. The best way to establish your leadership role and determine the basis for all behavior is to teach him that the way to get what he wants in life is to obey you. Break your training foundation once - even early on - and you have communicated that it's okay to ignore the rules. You will both make mistakes, so above all else always approach every situation with tender love and care!

Early Socialization

The difference between a well-adjusted, calm, friendly, pleasant dog and a fearful, anxious, nervous, and perhaps even aggressive dog may be the result of successful socialization. Experts agree the development period between 3 weeks and three months of age is the time puppies are least suspicious and most accepting of new experiences. During this early age, exposure to different sights, sounds, smells, people, and other animals teaches confidence and helps your dog learn to interact in a human environment.

Exposure to new elements at an early age is another building block for your dog's life experiences. Somewhere between 12 and 18 weeks your puppy will move into a new period of development. He will become more cautious and guarded in unfamiliar situations. This reaction is a natural survival instinct. For this reason, the wider the range of different situations you introduce comfortably, the better socially adjusted your puppy will become.

You want your Teddy Bear pup to mature into a strong, confident adult. Begin to take your puppy on walks around your neighborhood. He should become accustomed to the sound of vehicles, other animals, children yelling, babies crying, and loud music - anything that is a part of your world. Inside the house, expose him to typical commotions like vacuum cleaners, hair dryers, mixers, alarm clocks, and the television. The more elements your puppy safely experiences early on, the more reassurance he will have to control his fears in later life.

Beyond the common situations, your dog will need to learn to respect the participation of other key people in her life. You should plan field trips to the veterinarian, the groomer, trainer, dog-sitter, and dog-walker, familiarizing her to a variety of different people. Take her to new buildings before professional visits are scheduled. She will learn to relax in a strange setting.

Handling is a big part of the socialization process. Touch your puppy and teach him to calm when his feet, ears, eyes, teeth, tail, nose, and every other part of his body is examined. Play with his feet and gently tug on each toenail. Hold him with his back in your arms or on your lap and stroke his belly and under his chin. It will familiarize the sensation when he is examined by a vet or groomer. If he objects to having a certain area touched, work through the reluctance by offering treats and slowly moving back to that part of the body.

Never let a new situation become overwhelming for your puppy. The goal of early socialization is to help your dog become comfortable. Overstimulation or fear can create an opposite and very undesirable effect. Make sure your pup knows she is safe, and you are there to take care of her. Praise, pet, and reward successful new encounters. Never scold or punish if she exhibits fear. Gently remove her from the experience and gradually reintroduce her when she calms.

One effective socialization experience for puppies and their human parent is a puppy kindergarten class. Many retail pet stores and community centers offer beginner classes on a regular basis. Check with local store listings, veterinarian offices, groomers, or the American Kennel Club for class locations and contact information.

It is wise to consider vaccinations before you take your pup to dog parks or areas where he may be exposed to communicable canine diseases. Consult with your dog's health care provider and evaluate appropriate risk areas to avoid. Locations that offer great social exposure with minimal risk include:

- **Mall entrances and pet-friendly retail stores.** People cannot resist a puppy, and your baby will learn strangers often equal lots of attention and adoration.
- **Club meetings for girls and boys.** Most scout organizations offer badges that involve pet care. Take your puppy to a meeting as a dual learning experience.
- **Car rides.** Your Teddy Bear will learn to LOVE going in the car, and you will accomplish positive socialization experiences as well as adjustments to moving transportation.
- **Puppy play sessions.** Plan time for your pup to romp with other healthy puppies in a controlled environment.
- **Puppy day care.** Although most responsible centers require proof of vaccinations before they will accept a dog, puppy day care can be a great option for continued socialization as your Teddy Bear matures.

Teddy Bears are people magnets. It is nearly impossible to take one out anywhere without drawing a crowd of fawning fans.

WebMD provides this great socialization evaluation list for new pet owners. By checking experiences off the chart, you ensure a balanced and well-socialized start for your Teddy Bear.

Social Exposure at 8 to 16 weeks

EXPOSURE TO:	8	9	10	11	12	13	14	15	16
Babies, toddlers, children									
Teenagers, adults, elderly people									
People with wheelchairs, crutches									
In-line skaters, cyclists, skateboarders									
Drunk people, people with odd gaits									
People in uniform, veterinarians									
Repair people, delivery people									
People with umbrellas, helmets, masks									
People with hats, beards, glasses									
People with parcels, capes, sacks									

People with strollers, wagons

People of various ethnicities

Kids at school grounds

Crowds, clapping, cheering

People yelling, loud speakers

People dancing, singing

Livestock, waterfowl

Other puppies, friendly adult dogs

Other pets

Traffic, busses, trains, motorcycles

Boats, jet skis, snow mobiles

Manhole covers, grates

Shiny floors, tiles, icy streets

Gravel, cement, mud

Revolving signs, swinging bridges

Walks after dark, in bad weather

Hot air balloons & airplanes

Lawn mowers

Elevators, automatic doors

Balconies, stairs

Drive-thru's, car washes, tunnels

Electrical appliances, washers

Vacuum cleaners, hair dryers

Construction and machinery noises

Wind, rain, thunder, snow

Fireworks, sporting events, fairs

Veterinary hospitals and clinics

Thousands of dogs are abandoned, left at shelters, and even euthanized because of fearful, aggressive, and anti-social behavior. The need to socialize your puppy early and effectively cannot be over-stressed! Exposure to a wide range of experiences at an early age and continuing through his entire life provides his greatest chance at becoming the confident, well-adjusted dog you desire.

Treats and Rewards vs. Punishment

Spare the rod and spoil the dog? When you adopt any animal, you assume the responsibility of that pet's impact on your home and family as well as the community. Every day is a learning experience for the pet and the owner. Dogs are especially wired to observe, commit, and exercise their lessons. You must teach acceptable behaviors and correct unacceptable ones.

Teddy Bear dogs are smart. Their cute compact bodies and animated personalities tend to charm many people into forgiveness of the most blatant crimes. Still, it is in your puppy's best interest and for the benefit of the entire household that you develop standards for living as a member of the family. Some rules need to be made perfectly clear:

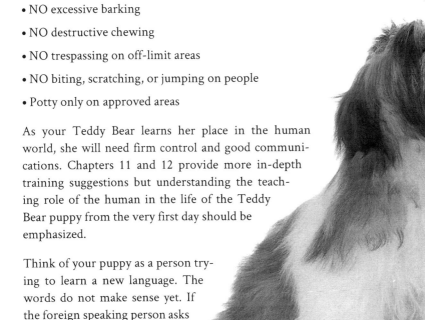

• NO excessive barking

• NO destructive chewing

• NO trespassing on off-limit areas

• NO biting, scratching, or jumping on people

• Potty only on approved areas

As your Teddy Bear learns her place in the human world, she will need firm control and good communications. Chapters 11 and 12 provide more in-depth training suggestions but understanding the teaching role of the human in the life of the Teddy Bear puppy from the very first day should be emphasized.

Think of your puppy as a person trying to learn a new language. The words do not make sense yet. If the foreign speaking person asks for a glass of agua and points to the faucet, you assume they want water. It the next time they ask for pan and point to the faucet you may be confused. Your dog experiences the same type of confusion when you scold him for a behavior only to let it pass the next time, and then scold the following time.

Regardless of your training style and approach, the key dictate is consistency! Establish your house rules the day your puppy arrives and stick to the program, no matter how difficult.

There is debate among expert trainers regarding the effectiveness of rewards-based versus punishment-based training. Either way, the immediate outcome for both techniques is the same - changing a behavior. The method best for you and your dog should be decided by the relationship you choose to develop with your Teddy Bear.

As far as your dog is concerned, learning exists by association on two levels

• **Repeat** behavior that returns positive results

• **Stop** behavior that returns negative results

Your approach to your dog's learned behavior manipulates his response. So do you choose REWARD or PUNISHMENT?

I'm the Boss

Training that utilizes punitive corrections is termed adverse-based training. This method supports the human's role as dominant or alpha. Your excited Teddy Bear jumps on you for attention. You shove him down with a sharp "bad boy!" You show him who's boss. Your reaction is natural and effective; you provide a negative result for an undesired behavior. Many would argue this type of punitive reinforcement establishes a fear-based relationship between the human and the dog. The bad behavior is discouraged by the bad experience. The dog fears repeating the action due to the pain he experiences as a result.

To work effectively, the punishment must be given at the exact moment the bad behavior occurs. The dog should reliably associate the action with the effect.

The penalty must fit the crime. The dog's punishment for the undesired behavior should be severe enough to mark the experience as negative. If the dog repeats the bad act, the punishment did not work. Measuring the exact dose of punishment is difficult, and every dog is different. For some a sharp "NO" or "BAD DOG" is enough to make the animal cower in fear. For others, a stronger physical punishment may be necessary. Escalating punishment can send the wrong lesson and often create worse behavior problems.

Will Work for Food

Many owners opt for reward-based training methods. Reward-based training can achieve the same results: encourage good behavior, discourage undesired behavior. Reward-based training is considered much safer, especially for new pet owners, as it does not cause pain or fear for the dog. Using rewards for reinforcement may seem to take longer when correcting bad behavior but it does not inspire fear, create stress, or promote aggression - all dangers associated with adverse training methods.

Reward-based training does not involve handing out a treat every time the dog does something good. The technique simply allows the human/leader to control positive resources to manipulate the desired outcome. By restricting access to the dog's desired resources then providing the desired "treat" when the behavior is accomplished, the dog learns the correct responses.

Like adverse training, reward-based training must be administered immediately. For example:

- **You give the 'sit' command** - your puppy sits on command, and you give him a treat and praise

- **You give the 'sit' command** - your puppy jumps and begs for the treat - you walk away until he calms and repeat the command. The treat is withheld until the desired result is accomplished

It should be noted that not all "treats" come in the way of food. A treat could be a chin scratch or belly rub. Teddy Bear dogs love their humans and have a great desire to please, but ultimately they, like all dogs, will base their behavior on the what have you done for me/to me lately theory. If an act brings the desired result the animal is motivated to continue. Likewise, an act that causes negative consequences tends to stop.

The first few weeks with your Teddy Bear puppy promise to be an exciting period filled with adjustments. By developing safe, appropriate ways to play with and hold your puppy, setting firm boundaries, initiating a robust socialization plan and a consistent way to reward and discipline behaviors, you will be well on your way to raising a healthy, happy dog.

CHAPTER 7

HOUSETRAINING

Your Teddy Bear puppy is settling in nicely to her human home. By the time she has eaten her first meal in your house, she has probably had at least one accident. You realize that one of the first basic levels of training must begin. If housetraining your puppy, teaching her the right time and appropriate place to potty, is not at the top of your list, one step in dog poop and it will be. Now it is time get down to business.

No Need for Privacy

Dogs are creatures of instinct. They work on the principle of "safe" or "dangerous" for the most part. Everything a human does to successfully train a dog can be accomplished by expanding on that basic principle, including housetraining. From the very beginning, you must balance the response to good behavior versus bad behavior by communicating "safe" or "dangerous."

In the Case of Housetraining:

• Your puppy pees on the floor - bad behavior. If you punish, you communicate that relieving herself here equals "danger" and you can create a fear factor that may cause worse behavior issues.

• Your puppy uses a pad or indicates a need to go outside to pee - good behavior. If you praise and reward, you communicate that the action equals "safety" plus a bonus - he gets a reward.

This method looks good on paper. It is an easier process than you will think in the beginning. Once your dog learns the appropriate place to eliminate he will continue the practice. It is much easier to work through the housetraining from the first day rather than ignore the obvious and suffer re-training.

Housetraining your Teddy Bear puppy, more than any other behavior, requires a solid system of 5 P's

- **PLAN**
- **PROCESS**
- **PREVENTION**
- **PERSEVERANCE**
- **PATIENCE**

As you begin, bear in mind that until the puppy reaches 12 weeks of age she has no ability to control her bladder. Most puppies will dribble urine as they walk or run. They have no concept of "holding it" until they reach their designated potty spot. That does not mean housetraining should be delayed, but keep in mind the limitations in the early stages of training.

Inside or Outside

Housetraining a puppy may seem like an insurmountable task. They can - and will - go anywhere! Keep the mission in perspective. You are attempting to accomplish only two goals:

- Preventing urination and defecation in unacceptable areas
- Reinforcing urination and defecation in designated areas

Work your housetraining plan around eating, sleeping, and playing. Keep your puppy on a consistent feeding schedule. Take the food away between meals. As soon as your dog eats, it is time to go potty. Introduce the verbal command of choice for eliminating and use it when you feel it is time for your dog's elimination.

When your Teddy Bear finishes her meal, wakes, plays, or drinks, attach her leash and say your cue word. It may be best to carry her outside or to her puppy pad to avoid accidents. Set her in a designated area and repeat the word. Keep her in the position until she has successfully eliminated. Praise her efforts-this is a training action that may not require a food treat. Simply making a celebration out of the success is enough to create positive reinforcement.

The first decision of your housetraining plan is where to establish the potty spot. Are you going to train the dog to go inside or outside? Most owners hope to train their puppies with dual options. Having a designated area inside the house is important if you are away for long periods and cannot get back to take the dog outside on the schedule.

Inside

There are a number of reasons to train a dog to eliminate inside. Urban dwellers without easy access to green spaces need to designate an inside potty space. Teddy Bear dogs are small and may be adversely affected by cold weather. Depending on the climate in your area, you may want to plan for an inside potty area exclusively.

The training principles for inside facilities versus outside are essentially the same. The tools may vary a bit. Instead of a grass surface as the trigger you will potty train on puppy pads, newspapers, or a litter box.

There are products to facilitate the dog's instinctive urge to eliminate. First, establish a specific room that is easy to clean up and preferably not carpeted. An area close to an outside door works well, especially if you plan to train for dual inside/outside facilities.

You should designate an area that is about 3-4 square feet. Consistently use that one area. Multiple inside locations will be confusing for the puppy. Decide on the best potty tool for your lifestyle:

- **Puppy pad**s are easy to use, disposable, layered pads. The base layer is designed to be leak proof and hold urine in to protect floors. The top layer consists of woven fibers treated with an attractant such as horse urine to cue the dog's elimination.
- **Litter boxes** are containers designed to hold cat litter, shredded newspapers, or sand as a potty. Spray attractants are available to encourage the dog's interest in and use of the litter box.
- **Newspapers** work like puppy pads. They do not offer the protection of layers like a puppy pad, and the dog may think ANY newspaper is a viable potty.

Do not use rugs as a potty pad. The dog will never reliably distinguish the difference between an old rug suitable for potty and a priceless heirloom rug.

Watch carefully anytime your puppy seems agitated, walks around in circles or begins sniffing the floor: these are signs that you should take her to the potty.

It may be necessary to use a leash to prevent wandering from the designated potty spot. As soon as she is successful, reward her with praise and/or clicker. Make sure she knows you are pleased with her action.

If accidents occur - and they will - do not punish your puppy. As soon as you see your puppy in the act, pick her up, correct in a firm voice, and say your verbal command as you place her in the right location. If she finishes eliminating in her potty place, reward her. Never rub your dog's nose in the urine or feces. If you find an accident and did not catch her in the act, it is too late to correct. Simply clean up, watch, and wait for the next opportunity.

Inside training can be difficult for some dogs. Others take it in stride. It may take longer because of the numerous opportunities for accidents. Some dogs trained for inside elimination are never able to achieve success outside.

Be sure to keep an enzymatic, urine/stool neutralizer on hand and clean areas of accidents thoroughly. Puppies will return to the soiled area bearing the scent of previous accidents.

Outside

Pet owners who prefer an outside potty spot will train their puppy for cues to go out. A dog's natural preference is outside, so by developing the system you are maximizing on an instinct.

Choose a designated potty location relatively close to the door. Plan to take your puppy outside frequently - at least every two hours during the initial training. Go immediately to the potty location and stay there until the dog is successful. Reward, then go for a walk or play. Make sure your dog understands that potty comes first, then play.

Be prepared to get up at least once a night to take your puppy out. They can hold themselves a bit longer at night as they sleep, since they do not eat or drink, and they are less active.

If you are planning on dual training, try to keep puppy pads or litter box next to the exit door. As your puppy becomes reliable at using the pads or litter box, graduate to taking her outside when she appears ready to go potty. You should accomplish inside training before adding outside training.

Don't Let Me Out of Your Sight

Successful housetraining means watching for clues - all the time. Puppies are not conditioned for schedules until well after 12 weeks. They will potty anywhere and everywhere if the urge hits. Experts use the general rule that a puppy can hold it - especially if crated - for about one hour longer than his age in months. So, if your puppy is three months old, he should be able to wait four hours between potty breaks.

Reinforcing desired behaviors and correcting behaviors that are not acceptable means catching your puppy in the act every time. We must be realistic; it is impossible to watch your Teddy Bear pup every minute of every day, despite the fact that you may want to. A safe containment area for all purposes will prove to be your best option.

Rewarding Positive Behavior

Rewards or positive reinforcement provides an incentive to do something right. It is a proven technique with animals and it works especially well with dogs. Rewarding your puppy for an action that you approve makes it more likely he will repeat the action. As he understands that the result of his behavior promotes the appearance of a treat, he will be most anxious to do it again and again. Positive reinforcement or rewards are a most powerful training tool.

Contrary to popular belief, rewards are not always food-based. The reward can be a toy, a pat on the head, scratching the ears, or even an attaboy! In the course of housetraining, develop a reward system that your pup appreciates. Try to use the same treat each time he is successful. As the desired behavior becomes more of a habit, you can reduce the treats but always reward with praise for a job well done.

Crate Training

As discussed in various chapters of our book, crate training your Teddy Bear puppy is a foundation for a good many other skills-especially housetraining. A dog typically will not soil his sleeping or eating area. Unless forced, they prefer to eliminate away from their beds and bowls. If you have established the crate as a den for sleeping, you have developed an excellent tool for housetraining.

Make sure the crate is an adequate size for your dog. It should be large enough for the dog to stand, stretch, and lay comfortably. Insert a cushion or rug and make the area cozy and inviting.

Leave the crate door open as you begin the training. If your puppy hesitates when going in, place a high value treat inside the crate. The treat should be just within your puppy's reach without entering. As the puppy gobbles down the treat toss another a little farther inside the crate. If you are using a clicker, click as he retrieves the treat. Otherwise, use a verbal cue like "yes" or "good boy." Do not close the door or force him to stay inside.

As he begins to go inside the crate for a treat without hesitation add the verbal cue, "go to bed." When he becomes more confident of the safety of the crate, you can close the door, but don't latch it. Let him settle inside for a few seconds then open the door, and he will come out. Gradually increase the length of time inside.

When your Teddy Bear pup learns to stay inside the crate with the door closed and without expressing anxiety, try moving away from his field of vision. Stay only a few seconds and return with a treat and verbal reward. Repeat the step, increasing the length of time he spends inside the crate. Always treat and provide a click or verbal reward.

Leave the crate door open when you aren't actively in a training session. Keep the puppy's toys inside, and occasionally hide a high value treat in the back. He will soon view his crate as a treasure trove.

Some puppies can adapt to a crate in a few hours. Others may express confinement anxiety and require the intervention of a behavior specialist. In any case, if your puppy is closed in the crate and starts whining or barking for release, do not open the door until he is quiet and calm.

Successful crate training is a valuable device. Do not abuse it. Never close your puppy in the crate as a form of punishment. Do not leave him inside for long periods of time. Always reward him for going inside the crate on cue. Never allow anyone to tease or provoke him in his crate. It should always be his safe haven. Most dogs will voluntarily go to their crate to sleep or if they are afraid of something.

Playpens and Doggie Doors

It is very important to adhere to a reasonable schedule for your dog's training, health and wellbeing. If you are away for 8-10 hours a day, try to find a dog walker to come in and help for the first several months. If arranging for support is not an option, keep your puppy in an exercise/play pen with puppy pads in the corner farthest from his sleeping area.

Playpens for dogs are available in a vast array of sizes, shapes, and price ranges. They may be soft sided, molded plastic, or wire construction. They are designed to fit nearly any living space based on the dog breed.

Playpens provide a confined space for your dog to play. If properly installed playpens keep your puppy safe when you are not available to monitor her activity. Dog playpens are portable structures that can be used in or out of doors.

Most dogs love their playpen. They can move around, play with toys, and sleep safely without feeling confined. Make sure you provide water if you are leaving your puppy for an extended amount of time. Never remove a fussy dog from the playpen. Wait until she has calmed before releasing.

Doggie doors are a great device for older dogs trained for outdoor, fenced areas. The devices provide the option for the dog to enter and exit into their yard at will. They eliminate the need to grab a leash and take the dog out when he has to potty.

Dogs adjust to the concept of the doggie door with ease. Demonstrate going outside and back inside a couple of times, and they will get the hang of it. Doggie doors come in a variety of sizes and may be customized to fit most doors.

Inspect the perimeters of the yard fencing regularly to ensure there are no areas your dog can escape. The doors are equipped with shields to lock anytime the dog should stay in or out.

Setting a Schedule

Successful training of any behavior depends on communicating to your dog when he has accomplished something right or wrong. You must be on the spot to immediately reward and thereby reinforce the behavior. Random acts of positive or negative conduct could never occur often enough to support training. It is necessary to establish a reasonable schedule and stick to it.

- Keep your puppy on a consistent feeding schedule. Remove the food between feedings.
- Take the puppy to his potty place immediately after eating, drinking, playing, or sleeping.
- Puppies should be taken to the potty immediately after being released from the crate and before they are put in the crate.
- Take your puppy to the same place to potty on schedule, or every time he indicates a need to go.
- Remember this formula: a puppy can hold it one hour plus his age in months.
- Following elimination, allow your puppy some play time. Start with 20 minute increments and increase playtime as she ages.

Accidents Happen

A well housetrained, reliable dog may still experience accidents. These are situations that occur that are beyond his control. Issues that may contribute to breaking house-training include

- **Urine marking** - when a male or female dog is about three months old they may exhibit the tendency to "mark" surfaces by depositing small amounts of urine on them. The causes of urine markings are debatable. If the habit becomes problematic, consult a canine behavior specialist.

- **Separation anxiety** - some dogs experience nervous, anxious behavior when left alone. They may soil the house during periods alone. Dogs with separation anxiety should be confined during periods they are not supervised. Consult a veterinarian if the condition doesn't correct with maturity.

- **Submissive/excitement urination** - your puppy may leak urine when excited. If you notice puddles or sprinkles during greetings, when she is playing, or when she is being scolded, she is most likely experiencing submissive behavior. Other postures to look for are folded ears, tucked tail, rolling over on her back, whimpering, and averting eyes.

- **Strange environments** - a move to a new house or location can provoke accidental soiling, especially if another dog has been a part of the new environment.

- **Urinary tract infection** - a dog with a urinary tract infection may deposit a small amount of urine outside his potty place.

- **Change in diet** - can upset stomach, causing uncontrolled urination and/or diarrhea.

- **Gastrointestinal upsets** - tummy aches and upset stomachs may lead to diarrhea and cause uncontrolled defecation.

- **Medical conditions and some medications** - can cause incontinence and loss of control.

If your housetrained dog exhibits sudden and repetitive accidents, consult your veterinarian to rule out medical issues.

Housetraining is a big step in your puppy's acclimation to the human world. As noted, the greatest accomplishment in the training effort is the human's ability to develop the **PLAN, PROCESS** the progress, **PREVENT** the accidents, **PERSEVERE** despite setbacks, and demonstrate the **PATIENCE** to lead the puppy to success!

CHAPTER 8

MAKING FRIENDS: A SOCIAL TEDDY BEAR

A tiny, animated, fluffy ball of fur with bright, intelligent eyes and a button face - what's not to love? Teddy Bear puppies are people magnets. Take them anywhere, and they draw a crowd of admirers. A socialization program for your puppy will not be difficult, but it will be necessary. While a sweet, friendly, well-adjusted dog is a pleasure to own, a dog that is not properly socialized can become fearful, nervous, anxious and well…anything but a pleasure!

What's Important

A dog's personality is partially determined by his or her genetic profile. If your puppy is friendly and outgoing, you will need to continue fostering the good spirit with socialization. Maybe your heart went out to a shy puppy hiding in the corner of the kennel; you may have a bit more work to overcome a timid personality in the social world. Either way, instilling confidence and the trust of people in general is a worthy goal that leads to a healthy, happy dog.

Teddy Bear socialization means introducing him to many different people, places, and things and coming away with a good experience. Successful socialization develops a dog that is well-adjusted in a human world. Many owners mistakenly think that just by taking a puppy to the park and allowing her to play with another dog, they provide enough socializing. It takes many encounters in different settings to properly socialize a dog.

The ideal age to socialize is during your puppy's "accepting stage" of three to twelve weeks of age. After twelve weeks, a dog enters the "survival" period and may be easily frightened and suspicious of new environments and people. A dog that remains afraid and timid may also become destructive and aggressive.

Plan to introduce your puppy to at least one new experience every day for the first year of his life (refer to the chart in Chapter 6 for suggestions). It may be a new person, a different sound, a new animal, or a building she has never entered. Try to take her from her everyday environment and control the new encounter as much as possible. You should not allow an entire preschool class to mob her at once, but one child at a time should offer an enjoyable event.

Work to overcome any anxiety or fear of different normal experiences that she may demonstrate. Coax, comfort, and reward her acceptance of new situations. Overcome any negative encounter with assurance, treats, and repeat exposure until she is relaxed and accepting.

Puppy classes are a great socialization tool. Puppy kindergarten courses are designed to assist with socialization - plus they are fun! They facilitate the communication process between human and puppy. In addition to the socialization aspect, puppy classes teach basic commands, and they establish a platform for more advanced training as the dog matures.

Biting and Play Fighting

Playing is an important developmental function in a puppy's life. As early as three weeks, litter mates role play with one another, developing skills to survive in the wild. Domestic dogs do not need the ability to kill their food or fight for their place in the pack, but; the inherent behavior remains a part of their DNA. So a balance must be managed to discourage bad play and encourage good play.

Watch two or more puppies play. They will roll, run, bite, growl, wrestle, and race. Throw a toy in the mix and a hardy game of tug-of-war ensues. The play is usually initiated by a bow - butt in the air and front legs lowered to the ground. A puppy may bark for the playmate's attention or offer a nose poke as the invitation to get the game started. Puppies play hard, and the intensity of the game(s) escalates as the dogs mature. Still, there is an order of fair play to the games. Once a pup crosses the line and gets too rough the other pup will back off, and the game ends. This is how puppies learn appropriate social behavior within the pack.

For the most part, puppy play is all in fun and harmless. Even growling and blustering is a part of the game. Puppy play can become bad if one or more pup gets too wound up or begins to express bully tendencies. It is easy to spot a bully at play. The other play-mate will almost always end up at the bottom of the fray. "Play bites" are more focused to the head and face and clearly causes pain. A dog that seems anxious or reluctant to continue playing may be experiencing the bully effect. When posture is dominated by one dog consistently or if the puppies end up on hind legs, locked in a hold, you should intervene and separate.

Play dates with other puppies of a similar size and age should be encouraged. When you adopt a Teddy Bear dog, your family will become the "pack" and the puppy will need to play games with you. You should learn the difference between good play that teaches valuable lessons and bad play that encourages inappropriate behavior.

Good play builds relationships between the dog and his human. It provides for physical and mental stimulation, and it establishes the role of the leader (the human). A few good games to enjoy with your puppy include:

- **Tug-of-war** - a favorite game for most dogs. Select an appropriate designated toy, NEVER a sock or piece of clothing. Hold the toy and let your puppy tug until he eventually frees it from your grip. Be cautious to not jerk the toy out of the dog's grip and damage teeth, jaw or mouth. When the game is finished put the toy away where the dog can't continue chewing. Tug-of-war builds jaw and muscle strength and teaches human dominance.

- **Hide-and-seek** - another favorite human/puppy game. Until the dog can reliably "stay" in the hold position, you may need two human players; one to hold the puppy while the other hides the treat. Select a high-value treat or a favorite toy. Hide the object then release the dog to "find." Dogs will also play to search for humans in hiding. Hide-and-seek offers the opportunity to reinforce the hold command, and it builds the dog's scenting ability.

- **Fetch** - what pup doesn't love the game of fetch? Select a toy - typically a ball - and introduce it to the puppy. Toss the object a short distance and instruct the dog to "fetch" then "bring it." Initially a chase will be involved, but with practice, the puppy will sit until the object is tossed, retrieve and return the object on command. Fetch teaches retrieval skills, and it is a great game for indoor play when the weather doesn't permit outdoor exercise.

- **Tricks and treats** - a fun game that can be played any day of the year, not just October 31st. Teach your pup how fun it is to learn tricks for treats. Vary the reward as the dog accomplishes the task. Teaching tricks exercises the mind, builds a platform for discipline, establishes good communication, and creates a bond between the human and pup (see Chapter 11 for tips).

- **Obstacle course** - can help your pup build skills for later agility competition. It is a fun way to train a dog around obstacles. Use furniture or set up baskets, rolled blankets, towels, and other things to create an obstacle course. Teach your dog to follow you around the course rewarding each time he makes it through without breaking the course an staying with the leader. Obstacle course training builds voice command training and teaches the puppy to heel.

Bad play introduces and encourages behaviors that can be destructive or lead to aggressive tendencies as the puppy matures. Examples of bad play include

- **Play fighting** - humans have a tendency to play rough with puppies. Pushing, shoving, rolling, wrestling play communicates that it is okay to behave in that manner. Puppies cannot distinguish between play and business. They do not understand why it is a game with an adult yet forbidden to play rough with a child. Rather than creating a conflict and encouraging bad behavior, DO NOT play games that include rough, physical activities.

- **Biting** - between teething and exploring their world via the mouth, a puppy's natural instinct is to bite. Playing with a five-week-old baby dog by allowing biting and nipping and experiencing the result of playing with a 1-year-old dog in the same manner can mean some nasty gashes for you. DO NOT encourage a biting game in any respect. If your puppy starts biting, stop the game and walk away. Stopping the play will communicate unacceptable behavior and encourage good habits as your dog grows toward adulthood.

- **Scare games** - participating in a game based on frightening your dog is dangerous business. Jumping from behind doors or furniture, grabbing the dog unexpectedly, or making sudden loud noises in an effort to scare, will compromise the dog's trust. You can create an anxious, fearful dog playing games such as this.

- **Laser lights** - these are often used to play with cats and owners will transfer the game to puppies - this is a BAD IDEA. Do not encourage your puppy to chase random lights. It may result in the dog chasing headlights, shadows, or other animals. Laser lights have also been known to cause seizures in some animals.

- **Keep away** - games that tease a dog such as keep away may teach traits including jumping, barking and snapping. Never permit anyone to tease your puppy-even in play.

All games with your Teddy Bear should be clearly started and ended by the human.

Playtime with your puppy should be a special, enjoyable experience. Devise games to teach good behaviors that will build your dog's character as an adult. Discourage any play activity that could be unhealthy, confusing, or dangerous, or that might encourage a bad habit that will prove difficult to overcome as your dog matures.

Is My Dog Too Timid or Too Aggressive?

Certain miniature and toy breeds have the reputation of being timid or shy. Some Teddy Bear pups may have inherited this trait from their parents. Concern about your puppy's personality is natural. Remember, puppies - like human children - move through phases of development. Shy behavior may be a part of a natural stage of your Teddy Bear's maturity. Still, there are measures owners can take to overcome shy behavior and ensure a confident, friendly dog.

Observe your puppy during socialization sessions. If she appears reluctant, shy, or scared, remove her from the situation. Ease her back in slowly and calmly. Coax her to relax and show her there is nothing to fear. Certain breeds can be more fearful of certain experiences than others. Never force a dog into a situation if they demonstrate high anxiety.

Never punish a dog for being fearful. Punishment only confirms the danger principle.

A shy, introverted dog may require more treats and praise during socialization. It is okay to offer rewards until the dog appears consistently comfortable with a new experience.

A timid, fearful, shy dog will be more likely to snap or bite if he is afraid. Use caution and watch for signs of stress: whining, submissive urination, panting, salivating, or yawning. Remove the dog from the experience immediately and try again when she is calm.

Consult a professional if the condition continues without improvement as your dog gets older.

A shy, timid dog can become a confident, loving pet. They may lack the exuberance of an extraverted animal in a new situation but with a little extra patience they will become a devoted, trusted, and loving companion.

Puppies may become aggressive as a result of fear, abuse, or other environmental issues. Some breeds have the reputation of being "aggressive" by nature. Few Teddy Bear dogs have the genetic disposition to be considered aggressive by breeding. It is extremely important to enter a consistent training program if your puppy demonstrates aggressive tendencies.

Aggression may be one of the most common behavior concerns in dogs. It sends owners seeking professional help from behaviorists and veterinarians. It is the reason many dogs end up in shelters. The sweet puppy suddenly turns mean!

The traits that indicate a possibly aggressive dog include the following:

- Growling

- Lunging or charging at a person or another animal

- Becoming still, rigid, or menacing

- Baring teeth

- Nipping

- Biting

An aggressive dog is not pleasant. Any dog will protect himself and/or their family, but a dog that expresses hostile behavior without being provoked may become dangerous. An isolated incident does not mean a dog is "aggressive." Repeated, unprovoked, random acts of aggressive behavior may indicate a serious problem. In order to help the animal overcome aggressive behavior, it is essential to understand the cause. Evaluate the situation and try to determine a pattern.

Puppies may appear more aggressive during the survival phase of development than any other time. They may react if provoked by an action they perceive as threatening, such as:

- Removing a food bowl

- Taking away a favorite toy or bone

- Disturbing the dog while sleeping

- Grabbing the dog expectantly even out of affection

- Manipulating the dog into a submissive or trapped position (forcing her on her back)

- Hitting or slapping the dog

- Playing rough with another family member

- Being examined by a veterinarian or groomer

- Crowding or pushing the dog

Social aggression usually appears between one and three years of age. Regardless of the root cause, any aggressive act must be addressed and corrected immediately. Seek the advice of experts if your Teddy Bear exhibits signs of consistent aggression. There may be a medical reason for such action. A behaviorist or other animal care professional can help plan a training program to get your puppy back on track.

I'm the Guard Dog - Puppy Communications 101

The foundation stock for most Teddy Bear dogs (Bichon Frisé, Toy Poodle, and Shih Tzu) carry four similar breed tendencies:

- Friendly

- High energy

- Affectionate

- Tend to bark often

The Bichon Frisé, Shih Tzu and toy Poodle were all at one time in their breed development used as guard dogs. Not the "fight-a-predator" kind of guarding, but an animal that could sound an alarm if intruders were about. There is a genetic tendency for the breeds to bark, and that tendency may carry to the hybrid Teddy Bear dogs. Obsessive barking can also be related to a condition affecting small/toy dogs known as *small dog syndrome.*

People talk, babies cry, dogs bark. The ability to make a sound is a basic communication tool. Some barking is good and certainly healthy. But too much of a good thing is annoying and will become a bad behavior. In order to develop a dog that is consistently good at barking for communication versus an obsessive barker, you need to understand why your dog is barking and be ready to reward positive behavior and correct negative.

Stranger danger is a type of bark your dog will use if there are people or other animals around your property. The doorbell rings and he knows that typically means strangers, so the barking commences. Stranger danger warning barks are loud, sharp, and insistent. It is good communication intended to protect your home, family, and property.

Anxious barking is a coping mechanism your dog will use if she is scared or lonely. This type of barking is typically higher pitched and may include howling or whining. Anxious barking is good if it tells you the dog is scared and she quietens when the danger passes. If anxious barking is a part of another behavior issue like separation anxiety, correction will be necessary or it could become obsessive barking.

Playful barking is usually animated and friendly. You puppy will bark when she is having a good time. Playful barking means fun, and it typically does not become obsessive.

Here I am barking. Your Teddy Bear may bark to get your attention. He is saying, *"Hey, look at me!"* This type of bark is also distinct and easy to understand.

Greeting barking. It is very common for a dog to bark in response to other dogs. It is a social connection, their way of saying, *"Hey, dawg!"*

Confinement barking. A dog that is confined will often bark out of frustration or boredom. They are saying, *"Get me the heck out of here!"*

Learning to communicate and control your dog's tendency to bark will establish a good bond and help you socialize your puppy. With observation, patience, and training, he will become a good dog that is appreciated by your neighbors.

Behavior Around Other Dogs

Socialization for your Teddy Bear puppy involves interaction with people and places, but a big element is socialization with other dogs.

Dogs have a very complicated hierarchy. As you learn to communicate with your Teddy Bear you will be able to spot certain mannerisms and understand his reactions. Closely watching your dog for signs of fear or anxiety will be especially important when he is introduced to new dogs.

A few tips for proper introductions may help your puppy develop confident, friendly behavior around other dogs.

Always leash - Small dogs like Teddy Bears are at risk of being injured by a bigger dog. It is always a good idea to keep your dog on a leash when she is exposed to new dogs. Most communities have leash laws, so any other dog you encounter should also be leashed. If you approach a strange dog that is not on a leash, it is a good idea to move in another direction.

Approach - Keep the leash taut when approaching another dog. Puppies are especially enthusiastic and may frighten another dog. Puppies live by the *"I'm the baby; you've gotta love me"* perception. Often, other dogs will not see the attraction, so control the first meeting to the best degree possible.

Introduce - Let the dogs touch noses and sniff one another briefly. Do not let the smelling continue for too long as it can become combative. Provide a treat for both dogs, indicating *"well done!"*

Body language - watch for cues from both dogs. A playful "bow" from one of the dogs is a good indication of an invitation to play. If there is growling, teeth-baring, standing very still, staring, or hair standing along either dog's back, move away. Move slowly and try a diversion before you move. Drop a treat, give a "sit" command, or begin happy talk. Do not jerk your puppy away suddenly as it can provoke an attack. It doesn't mean the two dogs will never get along; in fact, you may try introductions again as the situation calms.

Not all dogs have the advantage of good training and socialization. It is your responsibility to watch for red flags and remove your dog from bad situations. Not all socialization events will provide positive experiences so be prepared to overcome any negative outcome. Teaching your puppy the value of experiencing other people, places and things will make his life in the human world safe, comfortable and happy.

CHAPTER 9

BEING A PUPPY PARENT

Holding Your Teddy Bear to Dog Standards

Teddy Bear puppies are among the cutest, most charming critters you could ever choose to be a part of your life. And as such, some owners let them get away with a lot! Before you ever bring home one of these wriggling balls of enthusiasm, it is important to plan how exactly you are going to channel their energy. Teddy Bears may be small, but they can be just as well-trained and respectful as any other breed. It just takes a firm hand from the owner, which can be hard when even the bad stuff they do is just so darn cute. Stay strong! Your Teddy will develop good habits for life, and years down the line you'll be glad you persevered.

Chewing Your Fingers

New puppies teethe, and when they do they want to chew everything. This is especially true of Teddy pups, who definitely have a mischievous side. When your puppy wants to chew on your fingers, this is not necessarily a good or bad thing. But it should be controlled. It is natural for your little puppy to "mouth" on your fingers while you are playing with him. You should focus on transitioning this behavior to better outlets, not forbidding it altogether.

When your pup is mouthing your fingers, make sure she's not doing this too hard.

Watch puppies play sometime. They are all tumbling and biting each other in play. But sometimes one will bite another just a little too hard. The puppy will yelp, and the rough puppy will be surprised. Play will briefly pause, and the rough puppy will have learned that what she did was aggressive enough to cause pain. Gradually, they get the hang of appropriate "fight play", and it is no longer a problem.

You should approach the situation similarly. When your puppy gnaws a little too hard on your finger, say "Ouch!" loudly and pull back your hand. Your startled Teddy Bear will know that something went wrong. If she bites hard again, yelp again, and make her stop playing. Eventually she will learn that a certain amount of jaw pressure is too much for play. Some experts think that dogs who understand this bite more gently in every situation, even if they feel endangered. Gradually introduce appropriate chews for your puppy to gnaw on instead of your fingers.

If mouthing persists for weeks and months, refuse to play with your puppy if she behaves that way. A little mouthing may be okay for you, and that's your choice, but by refusing to play, you reward bad behavior with a "time out". If you have to put your pup in time out, keep it short. Then re-initiate play and repeat the time out phase if she bites too hard again. This is especially true if your puppy likes to nip at feet and heels while you are walking. If this happens, stand still. By being still, you are no longer "engaging" the puppy and she knows that this is not how to get your attention. Take her nipping tendency and channel it somewhere constructive, like a chew toy. With a little focused attention, your Teddy Bear will learn what is appropriate and what is not.

Watch Your Legs! (Humping)

Humping, to some degree, is natural for all dogs, male and female. If it happens every now and then, don't worry about it. But if your Teddy is humping everything that moves, there are important steps to take. Mounting and humping can get your pup in trouble if he messes with a cranky dog! Luckily, there are plenty of ways to get him acting right in no time.

❶ **Get your puppy spayed or neutered.** There is almost never any reason not to do this. By fixing your dog, he or she will be less sexually charged and less likely to mount and hump. This doesn't always stop the behavior, but it is a great start. Some dogs learn to hump because they were fixed too late in life, associating the behavior with good feelings, so don't delay a spay or neuter.

❷ **Socialize, socialize, socialize.** Puppies naturally learn what kinds of behavior are appropriate. But to do so, you must put them in environments where they have to interact with different people and dogs. If your puppy humps the wrong dog, that dog will let him know in no uncertain terms that his amorous advances are unwelcome! After meeting many people, your pup will understand that people don't like to be mounted, especially if you intervene.

❸ **Distract, discipline, and time out.** If you've got a little humper, try to refocus her attention when she's caught in the act. Ask her to "sit" or perform another trick or command. Distract her with a toy or game. As a last resort, put her in a small, safe space, with no toys. Keep her there for two or three minutes, then bring her back to be with you. If she humps again, take her back to time out for a couple more minutes. She will eventually learn that, to be with you, she must practice a certain decorum. One last technique is especially helpful. If you have a persistently amorous Teddy, keep a short, light leash on her during supervised times. When she misbehaves, pick up the leash and walk her immediately to her time out zone. Never yell at a humper or punish them physically. Simple behavior modification works much better. Remember, your puppy wants nothing more than to be with you. If her behavior consistently keeps her from you, she will learn to do better.

Growling and Barking

It is perfectly natural for your puppy to want to protect you. But too much barking and growling can get out of hand, or can simply result from hyperactivity. While there is no "cure" for barking, Teddy Bears are not usually very yappy. If your pup barks and growls excessively, approach it very much like you would the humping above.

If you are in your house and your puppy is barking his head off, or growling a lot, even in play, it's time for time out. Again, time out should be brief. Your puppy will get the point after just a few times that, if she wants to hang out with you, she can't be yapping like a lunatic. This goes for growling, too. If your dog is growling out of fear, be compassionate. Try to make her feel safe and secure. Don't discipline her with a smack. Instead be very gentle and quiet in your discipline. Give her plenty of time to socialize and grow comfortable in the settings where you take her. This may take time, but she will learn.

If you are outside of the house and is growling and barking at strangers, use your leash to reroute her energy. If she is hyper-focused on someone she finds threatening, make her settle down. Have her sit or lie down. Talk to her soothingly and, if possible, let her meet the person or animal she found so threatening. Sometimes I like to carry a pocket of treats so that people that I meet with my dog can give her a treat, so she knows they are nice. If all else fails, walk her away from the situation or carry her elsewhere. Consistency, compassion, and discipline are the best way to regulate this behavior.

Digging

Puppies dig for many reasons. Maybe they are bored. Sometimes they are trying to make a shelter. Other times they become obsessed with real or imaginary prey. If your Teddy Bear is ruining your yard, you have to first figure out why he is doing it.

If your puppy is simply bored, he needs more or better quality exercise. These puppies enjoy focused play. Engage his mind with fetch, training, and tug. Don't be afraid to roughhouse with him a little bit. If you just put him out in the backyard and expect him to wear himself out, you can expect a certain amount of destructive behavior. If your puppy is old enough for unsupervised play in a backyard or other area, make sure he has toys to play with. Check up on him periodically, and supplement his time with attention-based play with you and your family. Also, take him for walks. This puppy loves to see the world, and to sniff everything new. Keeping your Teddy properly exercised and stimulated will go a long way in stopping destructive behaviors like digging.

Perhaps your pup is just hunting moles. If you have backyard pests, your pup can be your first warning. Make sure your yard is free from animals that might harm your puppy. Some puppies dig because they don't have any shelter in their yard. By providing a small dog house or enclosure, your puppy will have a refuge. Without a place like this, he may try to dig one of his own.

If your dog digs for the thrill of the dig, and cannot be corrected, make a "dig zone" in your yard. When you catch him digging, pick up your puppy and move him to this area. It will be his personal sandbox, and he can dig there to his heart's content.

Chewing and Shredding

Toilet Paper shredding isn't a problem for every puppy, but some Teddies love to "make it snow". If your pup is so compelled, there are plenty of easy steps to take.

- Just close the bathroom doors. This can be hard to remember at first, but with practice, you can eliminate toilet paper disasters this way. You can also keep toilet paper in a lidded container so that even if the door is open, your puppy can't get at the paper.
- Use baby gates. I think this method is great. It easily contains your puppy to certain areas of the house and keeps her from destroying things in forbidden zones, if that is her tendency.
- Buy locking trash cans. Some pups dig paper out of trash cans and reduce it to shreds before you can bat an eye. By locking the trash away, your pup won't be able to do it.

- Practice bathroom etiquette with your teddy. Take her into the bathroom and observe. When she goes for the toilet paper say "No!". Repeat until she understands that the toilet paper is not to be touched, chewed, or reduced to bits. If the behavior continues, keep her out of the bathroom or put her in time out if you catch her red-handed.

- Give her plenty of other toys and chews to work out her energy.

Separation Anxiety

This can be the saddest part of the day. For many weeks, my puppy would howl and howl when I went to work in the morning. I learned through observation that she quickly calmed down and went to sleep, but if separation anxiety is a problem for you, there are specific actions you can take.

- Don't make leaving a big deal. If you leave the house for extended periods of time, don't work your dog up before you go. She won't have her feelings hurt if you don't say 'goodbye'. Just walk out the door like it's the most natural thing in the world. It will likely become a normal part of your teddy's routine.

- Walk your teddy bear before you leave. This will tire her out a little bit and she won't be "on edge" when it comes time for you to leave.

- Start small. If this is a big problem for your puppy, take baby steps. Start by leaving your house for 2 minutes, just sitting on the steps outside with the door closed. Then return. Lengthen the amount of time spent outside the house until your puppy starts to learn that it's not the end of the world when mommy or daddy pops out for a bit. Your pup will eventually feel OK when you leave the house, and you'll always be able to enjoy your return, when your puppy greets you with joy.

Bolting - Playing Chase

It can be a very dangerous thing for a small puppy like a Teddy Bear to run off. This is a big reason why solid training is a must. You need to be absolutely certain that your puppy will listen to you, even if he is distracted. This takes practice and patience. Start small. Make sure that your puppy will come when you call and sit and stay on command in the calm of your quiet home. Reward him with treats, and make sure that he will do this no matter what.

Then move outside. In a few weeks, you should have the same confidence that your puppy listens to your commands, inside and out. Finally, add distractions. If your puppy is old enough, go to a public area like a park, where it is safe for him to be off leash. Pick an enclosed area where you know you could catch him if you had to. Leave a short, light leash on his collar to aid in grabbing him if he bolts. Practice your commands here, with people, squirrels, and dogs around for distraction. When he has mastered the commands in this scenario, you know he knows them very well. Reinforce these commands with practice at all stages of your dog's life.

Another problem is bolting during play. Maybe your puppy really enjoys being chased. Some pups can get out of control and bolt during these playtimes. It is important for you to send the right signals to your Teddy. If he is getting too wound up, bring the energy down. Pick him up, or have him lie down until he is settled. If he is acting wild, he may not listen to commands he normally would. It is important for dogs of all types to understand the difference between play and serious time. Dogs that don't understand the limits of play can act inappropriately and even run off. Give your pup strict time outs if she doesn't listen to your commands or runs away. Soon, she will know to stay close by and always pay attention.

Teddy Bear puppies present challenges, but they are smart and attentive dogs. With a little effort and consistency, your Teddy will learn exactly how to behave herself around you. With proper socialization she will learn how to interact with new people and animals as well. Simple, gentle discipline will go a long way toward curbing some of her unwanted behavior, and in no time, you'll have an extremely well-behaved little friend.

CHAPTER 10

LIVING WITH OTHER DOGS

Many new teddy bear owners already have one or more dogs. Teddies love canine companionship and get along well with most other dogs, but there are a number of things you can do to make sure you are setting them up for success. When placing a puppy into a new pack, you need to make sure the pup understands its social role. You'll also need to make sure your older dogs feel secure and appreciated now that you are giving so much attention to this new baby. With a little compassion and patience, you will have dogs that live together perfectly, with your new Teddy right at the center.

Introducing Your New Puppy

Some adult dogs love new puppies right out of the gate. But this is the minority. If you are unsure how your current dogs are likely to react to the new Teddy, prepare for a chilly reception. In my experience, the relationship usually begins like this:

- Puppy is carried in. Adult dogs approach, intensely interested, wanting to know what it is I am carrying in my arms. I lower the pup and allow them to sniff.

- The dogs appear calm but alert. I place the pup on the floor and it bumbles towards them. They react in mild alarm and dismay. "Why is this little dog here?!"

- The older dogs can be a little huffy, giving the new kid the cold shoulder, even becoming very annoyed at its puppy antics.

- After a couple of weeks, they begin to play and integrate.

- After about three weeks, it's like the new puppy has been in the house forever.

That's the broad perspective. But there is a lot more to prepare for. From the moment a new Teddy Bear pup enters your home, you must be very vigilant in your observation of its interaction with older dogs. Most adult dogs will never hurt a puppy, but they can become irritated with the puppy's lack of social skills. You may hear growling and see pushing from your older dogs, to fend off a persistently annoying puppy. Don't be alarmed at this. Growling is the way adult dogs say, "That's not how you interact with me!" Your puppy needs to learn, and there is no better teacher than an older dog. Remember, until the day you bring your Teddy pup home, most of its experience with play has been with its littermates. With puppy-to-puppy play, nearly anything goes. It will take some time for the new pup to learn the ropes of mature dog social behavior.

The only time I will intervene and pull a new puppy away from an adult dog is when the puppy is yelping and the adult dog is continuing to be very rough. A yelp is a puppy's way of saying "I give up!" Grown up dogs will often growl or bat a puppy to teach a lesson, and this may result in a yelp. But if the yelps continue and the adult dog is growing angry, this should not be allowed. The dog should be separated from the pup until everyone has calmed down. Then the dogs can be reintroduced to each other in a calm setting. By avoiding these scuffles, or by quickly shutting them down, you will make sure that the puppy doesn't fear the older dog, and the older dog knows it has to be nice to the puppy.

It is important for your older dog to be patient with the new puppy, but you should also be conscious of your older dog's feelings. The older dog may have been the only dog in the house, or in a secure social position among other dogs, for years. By introducing the puppy, the older dog has to give up some of its identity. Find time to give the older dog individual attention. Also, if the new puppy is driving it crazy, give the puppy nap times in another room, or give the older dog a special treat in its crate, away from the annoying puppy. This way, the older dog knows that you still love it individually. If it doesn't feel neglected or unloved, it will be much more willing to accept a new puppy.

After 2 of 3 weeks of steady interaction, you will start to see some harmony in the relationship between the Teddy pup and your older dog. Where at first they didn't play or the puppy played inappropriately (jumping on the older dog's head, chewing on its ears, etc.), you will start to notice more "mature dog" play behavior from the little one. This is learned straight from the older dog. You will also start to see the older dog acting much more comfortable around the new kid. After a while, they will likely grow close, or at least grow accustomed to one another. In a couple of months, it will be like they have always lived together.

Another good way to get your new puppy up to speed with the behavior of grown-up dogs is to socialize it with dogs outside of your family unit. This is only appropriate after your pup has had its proper immunizations. But if the puppy is up-to-date, interacting with new dogs at a park or another dog-friendly place is a great way for your pup to learn good social behavior. This also takes some of the pressure off your own adult dog. When bringing your puppy into dog park situations, be very attentive. It is not uncommon for adult dogs to be a little rough with puppies. This is almost always constructive, however. Your puppy will learn how to be a dog among other dogs, and these lessons will stick even when you get back home, making life a lot easier for your older dog.

Pack Mentality

All dogs (even your tiny Teddy) descend from wild dogs that lived in packs. Dogs of all breeds retain this pack instinct, and it can work for or against you as a new dog owner. Even if there is only one dog in your house, you are in that dog's pack. In order to have an orderly household with two or more dogs, it is imperative that you act as pack leader. Many dog owners assume that they lead their pack, when in reality one of the dogs is in charge. From day one with a new puppy, you must assert your dominance. A puppy that understands early on that it takes its cues from you will be a much better pet for years to come.

If you have multiple dogs, you will notice that size, strength, and age aren't the biggest factors in determining who's boss, among the animals. Very often, small dogs can assert dominance over much larger and stronger dogs. It's all a matter of attitude. A natural social order will evolve between your Teddy Bear pup and your older dogs. You simply need to ensure that you are seen as leader over all of them.

In the dog world, the pack leader is a dog that makes all the decisions for the group. It decides when the others eat, when they play, when they rest. It proves its ability to lead and never has to apologize for its choices. The other dogs recognize its authority and follow its lead. The same dynamic plays out in your household, but many owners find themselves too low on the pack totem pole. It is especially important for a new puppy to understand the appropriate social order of your house early on.

If you are truly perceived as pack leader, all dogs, especially the new pup, will take their cues from you. Feeding is a key time to express your authority. When it's time to eat, the dogs should not eat until they are respectful and quiet. Make them sit before placing their bowls in front of them. If one of them becomes protective of its bowl, growling at you if you go to touch it, do not tolerate this behavior. Safely remove the dog from the feeding area, gently scold, and put the animal in time out. Work with the dog until you can freely move the food bowl, even when the dog is standing right there. Similarly, don't allow a puppy to beg insistently for handouts while you are eating. Food and treats come from you, at your discretion, and a dog must respect this boundary.

The same holds true for walks. A new Teddy Bear puppy will need at least one 20-minute walk per day, increasing in duration as it gets older. When you leave the house, make sure your Teddy pup and the rest of your dogs are leashed but calm. Leave the house before the dogs and don't allow them to pull you along the sidewalk. By teaching a dog to "heel" you are really saying "I am in charge of where we go. You follow me." The new puppy may need individual attention in order to understand this. Make sure your Teddy follows well before taking it along on group walks with the rest of the dogs.

Finally, don't allow yourself overt favoritism among your dogs. Hold them all to the same standard of behavior. By doing so, they will more naturally fall in line, without feeling jealous or neglected. It can be easy to favor a new puppy, letting it get away with things your older dogs would be punished for. By giving consistent treatment to all, you'll have order in your ranks, and your dogs will get along with each other better too. In watching the dynamic between your dogs, old and new, make sure no one is getting bullied, being overly demonstrative, or feeling left out. It will take some work and observation, but within a few weeks, your new Teddy Bear puppy will be integrated into a functional pack that looks to you as respected leader.

Biting, Fighting, and Puppy Anger Management

It is only natural for a Teddy Bear puppy to roughhouse with your older dogs. However, if things leave the realm of play, and one or more dogs gets heated, you will need to intervene. When cultivating good behavior among your dogs, consistency is key. This also applies to fighting and biting. If your new puppy and other dogs recognize you as pack leader, as described above, they will be very responsive to the behaviors you endorse and allow within your house.

It is not uncommon for new puppies to obsess or "lock in" to certain behaviors. If your puppy grows angry or bites you or one of your other dogs, neutralize the situation. Scoop up the angry puppy and allow it to calm in your arms. Because a Teddy Bear puppy is so small, you should have no problem keeping it still until it has calmed down.

Stroke and soothe it until it feels happy and safe. Oftentimes, anger and biting can result from fear. Maybe the new puppy feels intimidated by the older dog. Watch carefully when two "problem" dogs interact, and intervene before anger situations develop.

Anyone who has spent time around dogs knows that sometimes anger erupts in a split second. If your puppy is having regular anger flare-ups, there is one solution that works best of all: the squirt bottle! Have a simple, clean squirt bottle, available at any hardware store, filled with water and at the ready when your older and younger dogs are interacting. When your puppy gets mad, starts snarling, bites, or shows its teeth, give him a few quick squirts. This is sufficient to surprise the puppy, snapping it out of its angry mindset. It also lets the pup know that you don't approve of temper outbursts. Teddy Bear puppies are very sweetly disposed, so this is not normally an issue. But if tempers do flare, have a squirt bottle on hand to set things right!

Raising Two Puppies at Once

You will hear professionals strongly discouraging introducing two puppies into your home at once, especially if the two are litter mates. "They'll get too close to each other, and not close enough to you," they say. "They'll cause so much trouble," they say. "You won't have the time or skill to train both of them properly," they say. And yet, in my personal experience, I have seen absolutely delightful pets result from two littermates simultaneously introduced to their family unit as puppies. It can be done, but I would be remiss to say it is easy. I would only recommend the adoption of two Teddy Bear puppies at once to a family where at least one adult member can be home almost all of the time, for at least a few weeks. The first month of a puppy's life at home with you is vital; all the more so when there are two.

So you really want two? Well, double the puppy, double the fun, double the work. Don't think that by getting two, you get some kind of time discount. These two will need individualized attention.

First of all, crate train them separately. Their crates can be side by side, but each puppy must learn to rest and sleep on its own, without the other one to keep it company. Double pups will inevitably grow emotionally close to each other. For this reason, it is good to maintain some distance between them at night, so they are most responsive to you, not to one another. There are a couple of crating strategies that may work well for you. If you start them crated side by side, gradually space the crates out until they are on opposite sides of the room. Then, ideally, move one crate to another room. You may want to do this from the very beginning, going "cold turkey" so to speak. Put one crate in your bedroom, and the other crate in another family member's bedroom. This works best with adults or older children who accept the responsibility of caring for a needy puppy, even in the middle of the night. By forcing both pups to depend on you and your family at night for comfort and care, both puppies will start to look to you for other needs.

You also need to train each Teddy individually. Simultaneous training is confusing for two puppies. If you are using a clicker, which pup was a single click intended for? Which behavior is being rewarded with a treat? Your pups will also be much more ripe for distraction in one another's company. For these reasons, train them separately or enlist the help of another training family member. The lessons will be much more effective this way.

It is important to play with both puppies by themselves. You can't do this all the time, of course, nor should you. But there can be unintended consequences if you always play with the two together. One puppy will always be a little bigger and stronger, or more assertive, than the other. This often results in the more assertive dog making rules for the more timid one. When fetching a stick, the one may always be the one to bring it back. If this continues indefinitely, the more timid pup may never be able to develop confidence, coordination, and certain skills. By playing with them individually, they both have a chance to develop at their own pace. When they come together, they can just have fun without you being as concerned about their individual development.

Take the time to walk and socialize both Teddies one-on-one. By walking alone with you, one puppy will be able to develop confidence on its own. It will also learn to rely on you as pack leader, not on a more confident litter mate. The same holds true for grooming visits, training classes, and many other social events for dogs. By forcing them to be self-sufficient, and sensitive to you, they will be much better dogs when you do take them out into the world together.

Of course you can't be expected to maintain two different lives for each dog. Nor should you. But you do need to give individual attention to both puppies, especially at the start. By learning young that you are their master, they will grow into great dogs, focused more on your needs than on one another. One puppy is a challenge, and two are all the more so. But this does not mean that you can be any less successful in raising two. You'll just have to give more time and commitment to raising your pups.

CHAPTER 11

TRAINING YOUR TEDDY BEAR PUPPY

The appropriate age to begin training your Teddy Bear puppy is as soon as you lift him or her into your arms. Some form of training ensues at that first connection. Training is a form of communication, and when you hold your puppy, you speak the universal language of love. Even a tiny puppy understands, "I love you and I will promise to protect you."

The process for effective training should be considered at each stage of your puppy's development. Plan your program and work your plan. Training your puppy is expanding your means of communication. The course should be fun and enjoyable. Exercise patience, affection, and persistence at all times.

Firm and Consistent Training

Try to schedule a period of time each day to work exclusively with your puppy. An ideal period is just before his meal. It is easier to hold the dog's attention if he is a little hungry and he will be most interested in earning food rewards for success.

The most important word he will learn is "NO." Teach him that command in the very beginning. Make sure he understands that you mean it when you say no. There are no alternatives and use a firm tone when you tell him no. When you say no, do not allow him the option of going forward with the activity. You must deliver the command with enough force to prevent the action. Someday that command could save his life.

You will need to train yourself to deliver the same messages in a consistent manner each time. Allowing variety in your messaging will tend to confuse the puppy and complicate the training.

It isn't fair to permit your dog to jump on you one time and reprimand him for jumping another time. The same thing is true of other family members. Make sure everyone who comes in contact with your Teddy Bear understands and obeys the same rules.

Benefits of a Well-Trained Puppy

Regardless of how old your dog is when you adopt, a good, consistent training program geared toward developing a well-adjusted, obedient dog is priceless. Training provides the foundation for the way your dog fits your family.

A well-trained dog participates with the family; he goes on trips, greets guests, and plays with kids. He is a trusted companion and welcomed at most events. There are few gifts as special as a dog that becomes a beloved neighbor in the community because of his or her exemplary behavior.

Studies indicate that training is the number one contributor to a dog remaining in a forever home versus ending up in a shelter. In the event that a dog has to be surrendered, training can mean the difference between being adopted or put down.

Training your dog not only develops strong communication lines; it establishes a bond, builds trust, enhances your relationship, and enriches the life you share with the best friend you could ever have.

Training a dog develops untapped character - in your dog and in you. The bonus leaves you with a good canine citizen for life!

Operant Conditioning Basics

It isn't necessary to hold a Ph.D. in dog psychology to learn to train your puppy. A brief overview of various theories of canine conditioning may help you choose a plan as you look at different methods. Follow the techniques of a celebrity trainer like Cesar Millan or Victoria Stilwell, and you will implement some form of psychological conditioning.

A basic technique in canine training involves operant conditioning. The term is used to describe the cause and effect of a training action. Essentially, operant conditioning works on the principle that behavior is the product of the consequence. In other words, your dog carries out an action because of what happens after he does it.

You give the command to "sit" and your dog obeys - you provide a treat and a hearty "good boy." You give the command "sit" and your dog enthusiastically jumps up on you in search of a treat - you say "no" and turn away. Both situations represent an example of operant conditioning. Using the theory of operant conditioning you may reward your dog when he carries out a command successfully or punish him for a bad behavior by withholding what he wants. Each method builds reinforcement of an action with an appropriate response after the action.

Classical conditioning and vicarious conditioning are also training methods, but operant conditioning is by far the easiest and most effective application used to shape a canine's behavior. Methods included in operant conditioning include

• Positive reinforcement

• Negative reinforcement

• Punishment

• Extinction

• Fading

• Shaping

• Stretching the ratio

Under no circumstances should a training program involve punitive, physical punishment or abuse. Physically hitting or kicking your dog, or using other violent actions only frightens the dog and breaks the trust bond with the trainer. Your goal is to establish healthy respect and obedience - not to foster fear and anxiety.

Primary Reinforcements

When reading canine training guides, you will no doubt stumble across sections involving reinforcements. Reinforcement is simply the method by which you establish the communication to tell your dog, "Attaboy, keep doing that!"

Primary reinforcements are typically rewards of some sort. They provide gratification for your dog's positive behavior. The use of primary reinforcements is considered more effective in changing behavior than the use of negative reinforcement or punishment.

Your dog bolts out the door each time the door opens. Your dog learns the "sit" and "stay" positions. Put the dog in the "stay" position and open the door. Each time the dog holds the position and resists the urge to rush outside, you provide a high-value treat. Eventually, the desire to get the treat will outweigh the urge to race outside and your dog will reliably wait until you give the release command to "go out." If you are working to change your dog's behavior, you may find primary reinforcement methods most successful.

Secondary Reinforcements

A secondary reinforcement is a signal used to establish a backup to the primary reinforcement. Trainers who utilize hand signals, clickers, whistles, or other audible signals when training are developing the reward method of secondary reinforcement. Secondary reinforcement depends on effectively executing the sequence for the dog to understand that his action was good.

Your dog is working on the "stay" or "wait" command. You put the dog in a hold position (sitting or lying down). Walk away from the dog, and he holds the position. You release, click, and simultaneously provide a high-value treat. The dog soon associates the click with GOOD!

When training with secondary reinforcements, it is essential to use the SAME reward signal for each successful action.

Food Lures

It doesn't take long for the owner to understand that the way to his puppy's heart (or head) is through his stomach. Many dogs will do nearly anything for a treat. It is important when developing a consistent training program to depend on a variety of rewards - not just yummy food treats.

Food lures establish a quick way to get your dog's attention. They represent a physical reward for exercising a desired behavior. Food will do two things:

❶ Teach the meaning of a command
❷ Teach the result of success

Using food lures exclusively has a negative side. Too many food treats can contribute to an overweight dog. Using high-value food treats (like hot dogs or cheese) can compromise the dog's appetite for his healthy food at mealtime. Perhaps the most significant issue with using food treats is the dog's ability to slide into the "what have you done for me lately" phase. The dog may then refuse to work without a treat or demand only high-value favorites.

Even exciting, delicious snacks can become boring and lose their appeal. It is important to mix it up and assign values to the reward system. Anything that causes your dog to react positively can be used as a lure. You may establish your reward system to include:

• High-value treats: pieces of meat, cheese, bits of favorite dog biscuits

• Treats: pieces of kibble or dog food

• Verbal rewards: good boy/good girl

• Affectionate reward: pat the head, scratch an ear

Many expert trainers use the half dozen rule: only use food for a half dozen command trials. As the dog is reliably able to execute the exercise, phase out the food and use hand signals or audible cues for reinforcement. Developing a secondary reinforcement system and phasing out food treats is highly recommended for a healthy, consistent training program.

Small Steps to Success

There are steps to follow when developing a training program. The basics include four stages of a command:

❶ Request
❷ Lure
❸ Response
❹ Reward

It sounds simple, and it can be. Puppies learn fast. Most trainers will suggest a three pass key. Accomplish a task successfully three times in a row and your puppy will begin to reliably repeat on command.

Developing a foundation for training and consistent communications will determine the rate of success. Plan to train beginning the first day your puppy arrives in his or her new home.

Try to hold the training session at the same time every day. Before a meal is a great time as the dog will be most attentive-especially if food lures are used.

Make the training sessions fun and exciting. Do not create a stressful environment. If you are frustrated or weary or if your puppy exhibits a difficult time concentrating, relax, calm down, and start again. It isn't necessary to learn a new task every day, but it is necessary to stay on track with scheduling time and exercising learned skills each day.

Choose a training area that is relatively free from distractions to begin. It is most difficult to gain your puppy's attention if a group of children or other dogs are playing nearby.

Begin the program for your Teddy Bear puppy with basic, easy commands (*see Chapter 12*). Review skills the dog has learned using the above stages for reference; request, lure, response, reward. You dog will understand that it is business time.

After the review, work on one or two new skills per session. Do not overstimulate or try too much in one session. Even if your dog is an expert at grasping new commands, introduce one skill at a time and work on it until mastered.

When planning skills for your dog, consider his or her genetic/breed disposition. Chances are you will have an easy time teaching a Labrador retriever to fetch, while teaching a Dachshund the same skill may require more work. Try to build on his or her natural abilities.

Always begin and end every training session with success. Choose your dog's most reliable skill to start your training session and his best accomplishment to end the session.

As you and your dog become more familiar with the training program mix it up. Schedule sessions at different times of the day, different locations and add more difficult exercises. Dogs participating in obedience competition, agility trials, and even dog shows must be able to remain in a training stance during competitions and trials despite many sensory distractions.

Hiring a Trainer

It is an established fact that training is the best form of communication and bonding between the owner and their dog. No one can accomplish the desired effects of a canine training program as effectively as the master or owner.

Basic training should be a commitment much like food, health care, and shelter when a person chooses to adopt a dog. Beyond the housebreaking, leash training, and crate training, learning to communicate effectively with your dog is an essential function for a full, satisfying relationship. From puppy kindergarten classes to advanced agility course-work, you make your Teddy Bear an active part of your family and life by training.

While training is a 50/50 proposition with half of the requirement for success residing with the dog and the other half with the owner, there are times when bringing a professional trainer to the mix may be recommended.

The popularity of reality television shows featuring celebrity trainers points to examples of extreme cases of bad canine behaviors that require professional intervention. Hopefully your interest in hiring a professional trainer is much less critical. A few reasons to consult the experts include:

• A dog possesses a unique skill set that should be expanded. Celebrity dogs like Lassie, Benji, and Uggie had to start somewhere and with expert training!

• A dog with chronic, unhealthy behaviors.

• A dog that demonstrates phobic or aggressive tendencies.

• A dog that may enter specialized events: agility, show dogs, and/or scent training.

• A dog that may enter a specialized occupation: K-9, therapy or service dogs, or search and rescue.

Often a dog with special needs may fall outside the owner's ability to work with him. In such cases, it is always better to seek a professional who involves the owner and the dog's extended family in the rehabilitation.

Canine trainers come with a broad range of expertise. A person conducting an introductory puppy class may not have the training and experience of a veterinarian behaviorist (DACVB). It is important to understand the distinctions within the profession and evaluate the type of training your dog may require. You would not seek the intervention of a medical professional if you only needed help getting your puppy housetrained.

Discuss professional training requirements with your animal medical provider. He or she should be able to recommend the right direction for your needs. Most veterinarians keep a referral list for a variety of training professionals.

Ultimately, the program that works successfully for you and your dog is the RIGHT training choice.

CHAPTER 12

BASIC COMMANDS

L earning to train your Teddy Bear puppy should be a wonderful adventure. It will build a better relationship between the two of you. Training enhances your lives and ensures your dog's safety. It is the owner's responsibility to teach the dog to live in harmony in your home and the human world.

Why a Well Trained Teddy Bear Can Go Anywhere - Almost

Teddy Bear dogs look like your favorite plush animal come to life. They possess a natural charm and friendly nature, and most people welcome the opportunity to fawn over one. Add good behavior, and you will find doors open that often will slam shut on a dog.

People enjoy showing their Teddy Bears off at parks, fairs and festivals, concerts, car shows, rodeos, and anywhere else they can. The little dogs are so easy to transport: just pop one in a puppy purse or stroller and off you go!

While it is true that Teddy Bear dogs may be small enough to be carried in a tote, there are access restrictions in the United States regarding pets in public places. Unless your Teddy Bear is a service dog, and you comply with the Americans with Disabilities Act, he or she cannot enter public buildings or other venues where pets are prohibited. It does not matter if your dog is in a purse, backpack, stroller, or leashed.

Public places that serve food must restrict access to animals due to health regulations.

Any retail outlet open to the public that offers food products - even coffee - may not allow animals inside near the area where food products are prepared or stored, unless the animal is used for ADA service. There are some pet-friendly restaurants that allow dogs on patio areas or in rooms sequestered from the kitchen area.

Some retail stores welcome pups. Superstores like PetCo and PetSmart, most small pet boutiques, sports stores and outdoor equipment retailers often encourage pet shoppers. Shopping malls with outside entrances to stores will usually permit leashed and other secured pets on the premise providing that the animals stay outside and do not bother other shoppers. Some retail stores may permit dogs inside, especially a puppy tucked inside a bag, providing you request permission and the dog is polite and well behaved. Indoor malls, theaters, most amusement parks, retail superstores (including Walmart and Target, Lowe's, Home Depot, Sam's Club, and Costco), and restaurants unless otherwise posted prohibit any animal except an ADA service animal.

Planes, trains, and automobiles are also more accepting of polite Teddy Bear dogs and other small pups. Most airlines, trains and bus companies have weight guidelines for dogs in the passenger cabin. Check with your preferred transportation to confirm the restrictions regarding your dog.

The American Kennel Club offers advanced obedience certification for dogs of all breeds and mixed breeds. If your Teddy Bear dog exhibits the positive behavior, training, and good temperament to pass the test she can be recognized as an AKC Canine Good Citizen Certification (CGC). Canine Good Citizens are provided with badges, and they may be further certified as therapy dogs and other specialized animal companions. As a CGC a dog can participate in visits to nursing homes, hospitals, schools, and rehabilitation facilities. CGC dogs can even become literacy partners and work to help children read.

Picking the Right Training Reward

The effectiveness of positive reinforcement training techniques has been established. Offering your dog a high-value treat in exchange for learning a command is a fast and smart way to train. What are the best treats for your Teddy Bear training efforts?

Think of treats as money. You expect pay a lot for a highly skilled job and not as much for a menial job that requires little effort. So you must devise a monetary system for rewarding your pet.

Teddy Bear dogs are smart, enthusiastic, and eager to learn. If you make training a fun and happy event, they will view it as a treat by itself. Of course, dogs also have limited attention spans, so you must use lures to keep them engaged in the sessions.

High-value treats are usually food-based. Nothing is a treat unless your dog desires it enough to work for it. Designate yummy delicacies your puppy loves as your top "dollar" offering. Try breaking dog biscuits, cheese, bits of hot dogs, anything your dog loves. It is much easier to work with small bits your pup can gobble down quickly instead of waiting for him to chew up a large morsel.

Ideas for treats include:

- **Packaged treats** - pet food aisles of retail stores stock a variety of dog treats. Look for high-quality ingredients, and small, soft bits (no larger than a piece of kibble) and make sure your dog loves it!

- **Cheese** - most dogs love cheese. Pre-wrapped slices or sticks make storage easy. Just break off small pieces for training purposes.

- **Hot dogs** - are a quick and inexpensive high-value treat. Cut the hot dog into small pieces and reward sparingly. Most dogs will work for hot dogs when nothing else motivates. Be cautious; hot dogs are loaded with calories and sodium. They can contribute to obesity and compromise other areas of your dog's health.

- **Table food** - is discouraged in most cases. Human food may contain toxins that can be dangerous for a dog's consumption. Leftover lean steak, chicken, turkey, and fish can make excellent high-value treats. Cut meat designed for training treats into small, bite-size chunks. Wash sauces, gravy or seasonings off before you give even a tiny piece to your dog. Table food should reserved for only the MOST critical training commands.

- **Kibble** - is a healthy and easy treat IF your dog will work for food. Training just before a meal may be enough inspiration. Try a handful of his regular dry food. If he doesn't respond enthusiastically, save the kibble for the lower value rewards.

- **NEVER** - give your dog processed human food, candy, cookies, or crackers. Chocolate can be lethal for a dog. Some fruits and vegetables are also toxic, including grapes, raisins, onions, nuts, garlic, and any food containing xylitol. Refer to the ASPCA list of dangerous foods to make sure your training treats are healthy.

Often the art of giving a treat is as important a reward as the food. Always give your dog an enthusiastic *"good dog"* for a job well done. As he becomes more reliable at performing a command, you can eliminate the food, but remember to reward with a verbal *"good dog."* An affectionate pat on the head or chin scratch also goes a long way when reinforcing positive behavior.

Mix the treats up as you move through your training routine. Start the sessions with a skill your dog has mastered, for example, *"sit."* As soon as his tail hits the ground, be ready with a high-value treat. As you review various learned skills, rotate high-value treats with lower value treats including simple verbal rewards. When you begin to introduce a new command, go back to using high-value rewards.

You do not want your dog to fill up on treats and lose interest in training. Keep treats in your pocket or training bag. They should be close enough to be able to reward success immediately but not sight. You dog may focus so much on the treat bag he can't concentrate on the exercise.

Quiet Training = Successful Training

Few noises are more annoying to humans that the incessant barking of a dog. The annoyance kicks up several notches when it happens in the middle of the night - ALL NIGHT! If your Teddy Bear inherited the gift of gab and barks a lot, you will want to work on quiet training sooner rather than later!

Fact: dogs bark. To stop a dog from barking altogether is a ridiculous concept, and if it were possible to achieve, it would not be healthy! Dogs bark for many reasons: happiness, excitement, boredom, loneliness, responding to other dogs, and giving warning. You WANT your Teddy Bear puppy to bark for the right reasons, but you should control the tendency toward obsessive barking.

Quiet training is a method of teaching your dog to settle on command and resist barking. The best way to control obsessive barking is never to let it start. Once your dog has the idea he can bark to obtain his or her desire, the behavior is reinforced and it will be much, much more difficult to control. Successful quiet training begins at the first yip!

In order to control a dog's compulsion to bark, it is important to understand why he is barking. By removing the motivation, you may control the barking.

❶ Objects - most dogs will sit at a window or door and bark at things passing by. Animals, people, cars, paper bags, shadows - it doesn't much matter. If it moves, they will bark at it. To eliminate this type of barking, close curtains and blinds, or put your dog in a room that does not have exposure to outside movements.

❷ Attention - remember, your dog is looking for a reward for his behavior. Do not give him one; ignore the barking until he stops! As soon as he stops, give him the attention he's seeking with an affectionate pat. DO NOT acknowledge him while he is barking.

❸ Desensitize - gradually expose your dog to the stimulus that is causing him to bark. When he investigates the object and finds it not so interesting, he will not be inclined to bark at it. Desensitizing is not always possible, especially if his attention is drawn to a squirrel, birds or the UPS truck.

❹ Distraction - if your dog begins barking at a stimulus, distract his attention to another task. For example, the doorbell rings and the dog barks in response - distract the barking impulse by assigning another task such as *"go to bed"* or *"go to your place."* Reward the task with a treat.

❺ Exercise - physical and mental exercise tires a dog and makes her less likely to bark unless there is a good reason.

It may seem counter-productive, but teaching your dog the *"speak"* command will control barking. Using a high-value treat as a lure, encourage your dog to bark using the *"speak"* command. When she barks a few times command *"quiet"* and offer the treat right at her nose. The dog will stop barking to smell or eat the treat. Follow with immediate and enthusiastic *"good dog"* praise for the accomplishment.

There is no benefit of yelling at the dog to *"shut up!"* The more you yell, the more the dog thinks you are a cheerleader, and he will happily continue barking.

Approach the quiet training with an enthusiastic and upbeat method. An angry, frustrated, aggressive approach will only scare the dog and make the training more difficult. The goal is to help your dog understand that *"quiet"* equals GOOD.

Be consistent with the training. While quiet training may not always be in a scheduled or controlled environment like other sessions, make sure you send the same message each time you exercise the command. Instruct all family members to deliver the same message. If your dog gets away with manic barking some of the time and then he is asked to *"quiet"* other times, he will not understand the reinforcement. Successful quiet/barking control training is an all or nothing proposition.

Basic Commands

Basic commands establish the core learning foundation for a dog and his human. From a few primary steps, many advanced skill sets can be accomplished. Obedience and reliably responding to commands is important for a dog's safety. The result of successful training is a dog that will stop on a dime if given a strong command - a very important trait if the dog is chasing across a busy street or charging headlong into danger.

One of the most critical commands for any dog, in any circumstance is *"come."* It is important that your dog will obey and return to you on command, regardless of the reinforcement. The ability to obey the *"come"* without fail may one day mean the difference between life and death.

COME

❶ Begin practicing the *"come"* command indoors with your dog on a loose leash.

❷ Wait until her attention is focused on something other than you, then say the dog's name and command *"come"* in a firm voice.

❸ You may need to clap your hands, stamp your feet, whistle or produce some enthusiastic movement to get her attention.

❹ As soon as your dog reaches you provide lavish praise and a high-value treat. Use treats only until the dog reliably responds to the command *"come."*

❺ If he does not come on command, tug on the leash with increasing force and repeat *"come"* until the command is obeyed. It is important that your dog will come on command regardless of the reinforcement. The *"come"* command may one day save his life.

❻ Practice the *"come"* command often, in various environments and with different distractions.

SIT

❶ Dangle a treat in front of your dog's nose, then slowly lift your hand up until positioned just above the dog's head. Your dog should follow the treat by moving her head up. If she jumps for the treat, pull back and wait until she calms.

❷ As her head follows your hand up, her tail should naturally position toward the floor. If she doesn't sit, gently push the dog's rear to the floor with the free hand and say *"sit."* As soon as her tail hits the floor, reward with the treat and an enthusiastic *"GOOD DOG."*

❸ Repeat the process until your dog has mastered the *"sit"* command without your assistance pushing the rear to the floor. Keep working until she will sit on voice command.

When you and your dog have mastered the *"sit"* command you can move to the extension *"stay."*

STAY/WAIT

❶ From the *"sit"* position, extend your hand with the palm out, fingers up, and take a step back. Say *"stay"* or *"wait"* in a firm voice. Maintain eye contact with your dog.

❷ Wait a few seconds, keeping eye contact all the while and keep palm extended. Use only one word for the command *"stay"* or *"wait."* If your dog remains in place, you can release him with your *"all clear"* command and reward.

❸ As your dog becomes more reliable with the *"stay/wait"* command, extend the hold period and distance, you move from the dog. Never reward and never scold if he breaks command. Simply go back to the *"sit"* command and slowly build up.

LAY/DOWN

From the *"sit"* position, you teach the *"lay"* command.

❶ Choose a high-value treat. Hold the treat in front of your body. The dog will need to focus complete attention on the morsel as she follows it to the floor.

❷ Move your hand very slowly toward the floor. Your dog should follow the treat and lower her body. As she lowers her body to the ground, tell her to *"lay"* or *"down."* Wait until she is in the commanded position before you reward with the treat. Keep your hand with the treat on the floor until she follows the *"down"* command.

❸ Repeat the steps until she obeys the *"down"* command reliably. As she executes the *"down"* on your voice command, vary the length of time before handing out the reward.

OFF/DOWN

The *"off/ own"* command will spare your clothes, furniture and your guest's tolerance as you train your dog to avoid jumping on people and things. It is tough to break a bad habit so plan on offering good rewards at first. Training *"off"* will require keen observation since you will need to catch your dog in the act of jumping to initiate the command.

❶ As soon as your dog jumps on something or someone, issue the *"off"* command in a firm voice. Do not use the word *"down"* if you have trained lying to the word *"down."*

❷ When your dog responds on command and all four paws are on the floor, reward with the treat. It may be necessary to lure him off the object by showing him the treat as you give the command.

❸ Repeat each time he jumps on an object. Reward until he will reliably jump off on command. Make sure your dog understands he is following your command to get off the object and he is not training you to provide a treat for a bad behavior.

GIVE/DROP

"Give/drop" is another important command for safety. Teaching the *"drop it"* command is easy and can become a fun game.

❶ Offer your dog a favorite toy.

❷ Once she has the toy in her mouth say *"drop it"* in a firm voice.

❸ As soon as the dog drops the toy, reward with a treat.

❹ If the dog doesn't release the toy on command, wave the treat under her nose. **DO NOT** pry the toy from her mouth. Only give the treat when the toy is dropped.

❺ Repeat until your dog reliably takes the toy and drops it on command.

LEAVE IT

"Leave it" follows the same principle as the *"drop it"* command.

❶ Put your dog in a *"stay"* position either sitting or lying.

❷ Place a toy or treat in front of him a few paces away from his mouth.

❸ Say the command *"leave it"* while maintaining eye contact.

❹ After a few seconds release you dog with an *"okay."*

❺ Repeat until the dog can reliably leave the reward for longer periods.

WALK/HEEL ON LEASH

Walking on a leash means maintaining physical control of your pup at all times. Leash training is essential when walking your dog in areas where you are confronted with vehicle traffic or pedestrians, or where your dog may be tempted to chase an animal. Leash training lowers flight risks and the chances of your dog becoming lost or injured.

❶ Begin by introducing your pup to the leash. Do not permit using the leash as a chew toy.

❷ Attach the leash to her collar and allow her to wander about inside the house on a loose leash.

❸ Practice holding the leash while playing with a toy.

❹ Eventually work up to walking while holding the leash.

❺ As your dog walks without pulling or objecting to the leash, provide treats and include praise.

❻ Take the leash training outside.

❼ Dogs will become excited at the sight of the leash because it represents *"walk."* As your dog adjusts to wearing a leash and walking politely, add the sit command to the process. Teach her to sit until the leash is attached for the walk.

Teaching a dog to heel is different from basic leash training; when a dog *"heels"*, he is invisibly attached to his handler's leg. The dog is taught to walk in tandem with the human. A dog that is trained to the *"heel"* command will stay in posture on or off leash.

❶ Start by leashing your dog and position him at your left side, both of you facing the same direction.

❷ Have a treat in your left hand at waist level.

❸ Say your dog's name. As soon as you make eye contact, take two steps. Keep the leash taut. If your dog moves with you and holds position at your left side, praise him enthusiastically and reward.

❹ As soon as he swallows the treat, repeat the process, taking more steps as you stage the session.

❺ Make sure you reward so your dog understands that his ACTION was good. You don't want him to think that he is being bribed with a treat.

❻ If your dog loses concentration or lags behind, stop, calm down, and repeat from step ❶

❼ When your dog is reliably following ten steps or more, add the *"heel"* command after saying your dog's name.

Start and end each training session with a successfully executed command. Remember, you are building your dog's skills. All domestic dogs require the same essential elements to live a healthy, happy life: food, water, shelter, exercise, stimulation, and human interaction. Training produces dogs (and humans) that are physically and mentally fit, well-adjusted, and a joy to interact with.

CHAPTER 13

NUTRITION

Why a Healthy Diet Is Important

Your Teddy Bear may be tiny, even when full grown. But it is going to grow a lot during these first weeks. A high quality puppy kibble for small breeds will be just the thing your Teddy pup needs for steady growth. Small dogs like Teddy Bears have very high metabolisms. This is especially true when they are young, because they are growing so fast. Just think: your Teddy may grow to be 6 to 10 times its weight at eight weeks of age. You'll want a puppy food that can fuel that amount of healthy growth without giving the pup anything it doesn't need.

Your Teddy will need three to four small meals per day. A good rule of thumb is to feed your pup one ounce of food per pound of body weight. If your new puppy seems hungry, don't be afraid to give a little more food. These little guys burn through their meals in no time. With age, your dog's meal schedule will stabilize. In these early days they are packing on pounds of muscle and bone and developing their brain. Your pup has good reason to gobble down meals, so be prepared to feed often or always have some kibble on hand.

Another good food option to keep stocked in the pantry is moist or semi-moist puppy food. These foods are saucy and delicious. Your puppy will love them. While they don't have enough fiber or other balanced ingredients to be your pup's sole food source, they make a great treat or addition to dry kibble. Moist food also helps keep your puppy hydrated, which can be a problem for some small dogs. It's not a necessity, but your Teddy would probably appreciate you buying a can or two once in awhile.

Commercial Food

Puppy food is more nutritionally dense than adult dog food. Because puppy bodies change so quickly, they need more protein, more nutrients, more everything than full-grown animals. When selecting food for your Teddy Bear, pick a quality food made especially for small breed puppies. In addition  to being packed with nutrients, small breed puppy food comes in a smaller kibble size for tiny jaws. It is not necessary to buy the most expensive option. Just choose a food made of ingredients that sound like something good to eat. The first couple of ingredients should be recognizable, whole food protein sources: chicken, salmon, beef, etc.

Animal byproducts should be nowhere to be found in your puppy's food. The standards for what animal byproducts are "edible" are sometimes very lax, especially in bargain brand puppy food. Some brands have been known to include long-dead animal parts and other things that you don't want anywhere near your Teddy Bear. Likewise, cheap fillers like corn shouldn't factor prominently into your food's composition, or at all. These fillers fill up a bag of kibble at little cost to the manufacturer, without providing good nutrition. But they are difficult to digest and can even cause a little Teddy to put on weight, without being properly nourished. Good food will probably weigh more than the cheap stuff, and your pup will have to eat less to meet its metabolic needs.

I'm not one to tell a new dog owner that they must buy really expensive dog food. But a Teddy Bear puppy's tiny size and relatively low food intake seems a good opportunity to buy great puppy food that will last you a long time. We're not talking about a mastiff puppy that can eat pounds of food a day. Teddies eat food a couple of ounces at a time, so I recommend that you make sure those ounces are of a very high quality. With good food, your Teddy Bear puppy can grow big (or as big as a Teddy can be) and strong, all the while feeling happy, healthy, and full of energy.

Homemade, Natural Food

By prepping your own puppy food at home, you have the advantage of being absolutely sure of what goes into it. You may be much more willing to invest in quality products, for the health of your puppy, than the typical dog food manufacturer. However, with many well-regulated and truly balanced foods on the market, you should make sure that you have the time and knowledge to give your puppy as much or more nutrition than would be available in a package of commercial puppy kibble.

So you want to set out to make your own complete and balanced Teddy Bear food at home. But what does "complete and balanced" mean? To understand this, you will have to know the composition of a well-rounded small dog diet. Does this mean that you have to provide each component of this diet in every meal? Of course not. But each facet should be represented adequately as a part of food they regularly receive, every day or two. Because puppies are susceptible to nutritional deficiencies, I would urge the would-be home puppy chef to read the following dietary criteria very carefully, do outside research, and talk to your trusted vet.

Protein sources should figure prominently into your puppy's homemade food. But no one protein source should compose more than half of your dog's diet. Feel free to alternate or mix proteins, and serve them either cooked or raw. You can even give your puppy meat scraps from the table, as long as they would be considered edible to a human. Never give a puppy gristle or fat. Now that you've selected some good, varied protein sources, these should represent about 55% of your puppy's food intake. Give a puppy only lean meat, as fatty meats can pack on the pounds (or ounces in the case of a Teddy) without providing nutrition as well. Boneless meats (dark meat chicken is better than breast), organ meats like heart and kidney, and deboned fish are all great choices, but there are many others. Raw, meaty bones are a good dietary addition, too, but I wouldn't recommend them for so tiny a dog. A small puppy can also derive benefit from about one half egg per day.

Yogurt and kefir are dairy products that puppies tend to tolerate well, while providing good energy and growth potential. If your pup has trouble with these, switch to goat's milk products. But avoid very fatty dairy products, like cheese. Darkly colored fruits and vegetables are another great addition. While wild dogs didn't eat these very much, your pup will benefit from the nutritive elements as well as the dietary fiber. Starches like potatoes and pumpkin (your Teddy will love pumpkin) can be cooked and added for enjoyment and healthy calories. Many are the times I have popped open a can of pumpkin puree to mix into a bowl of kibble for my happy dog. Leafy greens and very limited whole grains can help round out the diet. Take all of these ingredients and grind them in a meat grinder or food processor.

Calcium, in the form of crushed eggshells, bone meal, or any other pup-friendly form, must be added to homemade puppy foods. Add 1000 mg per pound. That translates to about half a teaspoon of eggshell powder, but be careful when you weigh with your kitchen scale to make sure you get it right. Also add fish oil if your Teddy isn't eating fish: about 200 mg per day. Cod liver oil is another good kind of fish oil in this case. Plant oils, vitamins D and E, and iodine are all supplements found lacking in most homemade formulas. Do your homework well if this is something you want to do, and have a conversation about it with your vet. Making your pup's food at home is perfectly fine, but you do need to make sure you are giving the little one adequate nutrition. Otherwise, leave this to the pros.

Puppy Food vs. People Food

This is an interesting topic. People tend to have differing opinions about it. On the one hand, you've got the folks who would never once give their Teddy even a crumb of people food. On the other hand, you've got the folks with their Teddy perched happily on their lap during dinner time, giving frequent handouts. I would recommend a middle way, but you are free to do what you want. The only thing I would stay away from entirely is giving your Teddy Bear junk food. Chocolate may seem like a fun treat for your dog, but it's important that you never give your puppy any of this toxic people food.

Giving your pup a taste of human food can give way to discipline problems. If you supply occasional handouts at dinnertime, your puppy could become a dog that whines and begs around your feet during supper. Left unchecked, they can become very demanding, feeling entitled to your food. They don't do this because they are bad dogs, but because you made them feel that this is their right. My answer to this is that my dogs never get a bite of food while I am eating. To earn a handout, they must lay quietly at my feet or on their bed. Having waited patiently, I either give them a really tasty bite or let them clean up my plate after eating. I, of course, only let them eat good, healthy foods off my plate. No scraps, no bones, and no gristle.

I can't emphasize the junk food issue enough. Many are the dogs I've seen that have swollen to obesity, all because the dog ate foods that frequently contribute to obesity to humans all around the world. Don't feed your puppy hot dogs, potato chips, or fast food. They'll love it and gobble up every bite, but while a cheeseburger may not be a lot for your metabolism and frame to handle, that's a LOT for a 12-pound dog. By keeping junk foods from your puppy's bowl, you are helping them stay trim and fit for life.

Dieting and Obesity

If you do find yourself with a pudgy pup, this isn't the end of the world. This is rarely a big problem for Teddy Bears, and is almost always the result of inactivity and overeating. If your vet identifies your puppy as overweight, make sure that its food is low in carbohydrates. As stated above, the manufacturers who make the least expensive puppy foods on the market frequently accomplish their price gouging by stuffing their kibble with cheap grains. Teddies don't eat corn. Teddies don't eat wheat. But the cheap stuff is full of it, and your puppy will be too. These fillers can give a puppy all kinds of digestive problems. They also have a much higher caloric load. Your puppy will also eat more of this food in order to consume its requisite nutritional needs. The low nutrition, high calorie food model packs the pounds onto many pups. Don't let your Teddy Bear be counted among their ranks!

Of course, your Teddy may just be gobbling up too much of the good stuff, in which case you should reduce its food intake, after a consultation from your vet. Your puppy may also just need more exercise. Teddy pups are so small and active that they typically burn a lot of calories just bouncing around your living room. But they do need time to run outside, play time with the family, a walk or two every day. If your pup is a slouch, it'll be much more likely to become obese.

Obesity isn't an enormous health concern in and of itself, but it is a precursor to much worse conditions. Obesity almost always precedes diabetes and certain hormone malfunctions. Just keep the dog active and fit - no tall order with a perky Teddy Bear - and your new puppy will be just fine.

CHAPTER 14

GROOMING YOUR TEDDY BEAR PUPPY

A Teddy Bear puppy is a ball of fluff and, as such, it will need some grooming attention. Luckily, these puppy coats are simple to deal with. If, as your puppy ages, you want to get fancy with your dog's coat, a groomer can get you there. But Teddy Bears have the name they do because, when you leave their fur short to medium in length all over, they look just like little stuffed animals. The rest of this chapter is written with this scruffy, cute, easy-to-manage haircut in mind.

What Type of Coat Do I Have?

Teddies have either a curly or silky hair texture, or some combination. Their hair usually turns out kind of wavy, kind of fluffy. It's a very soft shag kind of coat, and it's adorable. They tend to keep their puppy coat appearance for life. The texture doesn't change dramatically, so these little fellows always remain as fluffy and cuddly as the day you brought them home. Teddy coats come in a variety of color combinations. They can have patches of black, white, cream, brown, red, and apricot, as well as other variations. Each coat is as unique as a fingerprint, and you'll always be able to spot your Teddy because of its distinctive splotches.

Because their fur is usually left somewhat long and flyaway, daily brushing is important to avoid mats. If you miss a day, don't sweat it. Mats and tangles come out without too much fuss. I like small ball-tipped bristle brushes for tiny Teddies. The wide-spaced bristles reach all the way to the scalp, but the ball tips don't scratch tender puppy skin. They feel much more like a massage. The wide spacing also helps loosen simple tangles without catching and pulling. Your Teddy Bear will appreciate the consideration and will soon grow to enjoy brushing, so start early.

When brushing, don't just focus on the easy-to-reach spots. Mats tend to emerge in the places we overlook, like in the "armpits", the lower belly, and around the ears. I like to soothe my dog into a relaxed state with gentle brushing around her back and hindquarters, her favorite spot to be brushed. Once deep in a brush-induced trance, she'll rest in any position I move her. Now I flip her over gently and start to work on her belly and around her arms. Not only does this prevent tangles, it redistributes oils along the surface of individual hairs, to keep your pup's coat shiny and healthy.

If your new puppy doesn't like brushing, just keep at it, but don't traumatize a little dog by forcing the issue. Brush a bit and give a treat. Praise the puppy throughout so it feels the motivation to continue. If your puppy is feeling stressed, just stop for the day and come back later. Teddy Bear puppies won't have nagging coat problems unless their fur is very dirty and ill-attended. After a few days of light brushing, your puppy will forget that it ever disliked the experience and will sit for you with no problems.

Bathing

Not every Teddy loves tub time, and this doesn't always change. But not to fear. They're tiny dogs and won't take long to clean. As pups, you can quickly scrub them in your bathroom sink.

First of all, buy a gentle puppy shampoo. These shampoos have very mild detergents that won't hurt a puppy's eyes or irritate their skin. They are usually only mildly scented because strong perfumes can bother a puppy. Just imagine if you had a thick flowery scent clinging to hair all over your entire body. That would be overwhelming! So pick something that smells good, but not too good. Then just lather and rinse. It's entirely possible that you might have brought home a water bug who loves bath time, but most pups simply endure the experience. Make it short and sweet, then reward them by drying them off with a big, fluffy towel. Then enjoy watching them wriggle around the house until they've dried off.

One way you can make a bath a little more fun for a puppy is by keeping its head dry. No dog likes a wet head, and this alone can ruin bath time for life. If your puppy's head is really dirty for some reason, put a couple of cotton balls in its ears to keep water out. If you've seen dogs run around the house, rubbing their ears on the floor after bath time, this is the result of water in the ear canal. It is, at least, irritating, but can result in an ear infection if the canal stays wet. Another solution for a puppy head that needs a bath is dry shampoo. Dry shampoos can be rubbed into puppy fur and around sensitive areas like the eyes without applying water. This can be done any time, whether you're bathing the rest of the dog or not. By bathing the puppy's head elsewhere, you may stand a chance of having tub time be a pleasant thing for all.

Trimming Nails

Nail trimming is another thing that your Teddy Bear may either hate or be totally ambivalent about. The key is to start young. From day one, play with your puppy's paws. Make sure your Teddy is used to having them handled. Some dogs are uncomfortable with this, but you won't let your Teddy be one of them. When the nails are long enough to cut, you should have no problem handling the job.

First you need to select the right nail cutter. I prefer the scissor-style cutters. They look like tiny hedge limb cutters, and close just like scissors. This is in contrast to the "guillotine" style cutters which some people like but I do not. I find it too difficult to gauge the depth of my cut with the guillotines, so I like my scissor style.

When you trim a puppy's nails, especially for the first time, you want to do everything in your power to avoid cutting to the quick, the fleshy blood supply portion of the nail. It's sometimes called the "living nail". If you cut through part of this, and all of those nerve endings, your puppy will yelp, there will be blood, and your dog will (rightfully) be much more averse to having you clip his nails in the future. I always have a little tub of "quick stop" on hand, as I very occasionally cut close enough to the quick for a drop of blood to form. But I do everything to avoid it.

With puppies, simply "tip" the nail by filing. You'll take off the sharp point of the nail without causing any pain at all. I like to take a normal cardboard nail file and smooth the tip. This keeps the puppy from irritating its skin while scratching. By only tipping the nails, you may have to cut a little more often, but you'll never worry about cutting to the quick.

How do you know it's time to trim? When you hear your puppy clicking around hard floor surfaces, you are hearing the nails strike the floor with every footstep. The nails are too long and should be trimmed. Left unchecked, long nails can give a dog foot problems, and can lead to infections. But you'd never let them get that long, right?

Brushing Their Teeth

Most dog owners neglect to do this, but brushing is important! Just think what would happen to your teeth if you went about your life as you do now without ever brushing again. You would have dental pandemonium, and the same can be true for a dog. Dogs have the advantage of having more spaced-out teeth than humans, but tartar and gum disease can set in just the same. However, these conditions are preventable.

Small dogs like Teddy Bears don't have as much space between their teeth as large dogs, like German Shepherds. As such, they need brushing more frequently. If you can do it, brushing every day is not inappropriate. You'll save yourself having to pay very costly dental cleaning or gum surgery bills at your vet's office in 5 or 6 years.

So how do we go about this? First of all, you need a toothbrush. A dog friendly brush, sized small for a little Teddy, will be available at any pet store. You can also pick up toothpaste here, in flavors your little one will enjoy, like fish or beef. Never use human products for this purpose. Human toothbrushes aren't shaped right, and human toothpaste will be harmful if swallowed (and a dog most certainly will swallow paste during brushing). For those of us unwilling to buy these things, a finger and a simple paste of baking soda and water will do just as well, though the paste will not be as tasty.

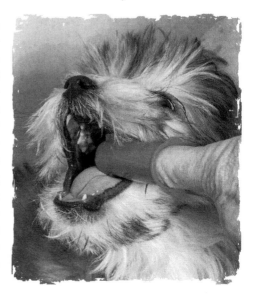

Let your puppy mouth the brush a little bit, to get used to the way it feels. Then let the pup lick a little bit of the flavored paste off your finger to get a taste for it. Then start brushing away. Gently work around every tooth, rubbing a little bit on the gums. If your pup struggles, leave it for a day and come back to it, just like with hair brushing. Gradually, your puppy will get used to the routine and will think nothing of its daily brushing. The same strategy applies to finger brushing with homemade paste. Just be careful with your finger the first couple of times you rub the pup's teeth!

In general, you should keep an eye on your Teddy's gum health, even if you brush every day. Healthy gums will be pink. White gums could indicate illness or infection. Red gums are usually inflamed with bacteria. If either seems problematic, or your pup's gums are bleeding, always consult your vet. Don't just try to "brush" the problem away. Generally though, Teddy Bears have good dental health, with only a little effort from mommy or daddy.

Cleaning Ears and Eyes

Redness also indicates inflammation of the eyes and ears. When your puppy looks to the side, you'll be able to see the whites. If they appear bloodshot, you know there's a little inflammation going on. This is usually due to allergies, but you'll want to mention it to your vet. Red ears can be troublesome with medium-to-longhaired dogs, like Teddy

Bears, but only if they aren't maintained. Take a peek into your puppy's ears once in awhile. If they are filled with hair, especially if the hair appears clumped or dirty, your vet may want to pluck some of it next time to prevent inflammation. Left unchecked, dirty ears can become infected, or serve as a habitat for ear mites. Because a dog can't tell you that its ear hurts, it is not uncommon for infections to go untreated, eventually damaging a poor dog's hearing. However, regular ear maintenance will keep this from happening under your watch.

Unless your vet specifically prescribes an eye cleaning solution, you should never put anything in your pup's eyes. You may occasionally see discharge or mucus around the corners of a dog's eyes, especially with longhaired dogs like Teddies. Just wipe it away with a rag or a cotton ball. This way, you can prevent the staining you see around the eyes of some dogs.

Talk to your vet about routine ear cleaning at home. If your pup doesn't need it, don't worry about it. But if it does, your veterinarian will prescribe you a simple ear cleaning solution. This solution is simply squirted into the ear canal. You will then massage your puppy's ear at the base, where it connects to the head, for about thirty seconds. Allow the dog to shake it out, then wipe the inside of the ear with a cotton ball or clean towel. Never use Q-tips or any other devices to clean inside the ear canal. Leave deep cleaning to your vet.

Haircuts at Home

You are free to act as barber to your Teddy Bear, and the job isn't a hard one. Teddy pups can usually get by with simple scissor cutting. If you are at all unsure with a scissor, make sure it's a safety scissor with soft tips. Then just cut the tips off the longest stuff. The ideal look for a Teddy pup is soft wavy fluff floating off in every direction. You can't get much better than that. You may also use electric trimmers with length guards, if the natural look is a little too long for you, or if the weather is very hot and your puppy would appreciate a fade.

The artistic can attempt more ambitious cuts at home. Because Teddies are a mix between Shih Tzus and Bichons, certain hairdos associated with each breed may be within reach.

You are free to do as you please. I offer only one word of caution. When using electric trimmers, be very careful not to cut the thin "web" of skin in your pup's "armpits". This webbed skin sticks out when your puppy's front leg is extended, and it's easy to nick, buried as it is under lots of hair. Once you're sure you won't cut this, feel free to give your pup any haircut you like.

Different Types of Teddy Bear Haircuts

The classic Teddy Bear look is scruffy all over, like a stuffed teddy bear. But the fur doesn't just grow this way, or at least it doesn't very well. It needs to be sculpted and shaped to achieve the perfect cute-all-over appearance. I am able to keep mine just the way I like her with a little scissoring around the face and legs. You may too, or you may want to employ a skilled groomer. Haircuts for little dogs like this shouldn't exceed $30-$40 at the most. For a puppy trim, you should only pay about $20.

You may want to achieve some of the sculpted hard lines of a Shih Tzu cut. Because Teddies are derived from Tzus, you can get this look to a point, but Teddies have curlier hair. If you try to mimic the balls of tight curls sported by a Bichon Frise, you'll find that a Teddy's curls are just too loose. A skilled groomer can test the limits, though. Me? I just prefer the Ewok look. Fuzzy all over, nothing too long or too short, shaped subtly with a scissor every week or so. It's adorable, and the simplest look to achieve with your Teddy Bear.

CHAPTER 15

BASIC HEALTH CARE

Teddy Bears are sturdy and long-lived. But, like all dogs, they need the occasional trip to the vet to make sure they're in tip-top shape. Since you have such a small dog, you will probably never have to worry about issues like hip dysplasia and arthritis that bother larger breeds. Teddy Bears also have the benefit of being a cross between two established breeds. Breed standards are difficult to preserve. The best breeders do so and produce very healthy animals, but less skilled breeders can cause future health problems by interbreeding dogs from the small pool of adult dogs they have access to. Mixed breeds tend to avoid these difficulties, because puppies come from unrelated parents. So do Teddies. Though an established breed standard, their blended parentage is an asset to their health. The issues I'll talk about below are problems that all dogs can run into. Your Teddy pup doesn't have to be one of them.

Fleas and Ticks

Fleas are the universal plague of the dog world. Even if your dog has never had them, you have certainly met a dog that does. Fleas are a problem that, once acquired, is difficult to solve. They can be really tough on your puppy!

Fleas are small, biting insect parasites. They are about as big as a sesame seed, but black. They can carry bacterial infections, which they deliver to dogs (and people) through their saliva, when they bite and draw blood. Each bite is noticeable and somewhat painful to your puppy, and the itch can be bothersome. Some bites become irritated until a rash forms. These rashes can become infected as the dog tries and tries to scratch the itch away. I once had to take one of my dogs to the vet and have her whole back end shaved. She lived the next week in "the cone of shame" to heal, even after her fleas were wiped out.

Puppies are especially vulnerable to fleas. Tiny dogs like Teddy Bears have thick fur that is a haven for swarms of the tiny parasites. Left untended, little dogs like this can actually grow anemic from the blood loss of dozens of flea bites. Even if the infestation doesn't get that bad, you can bet that your Teddy will be uncomfortable with even a few itchy fleas on board. If you think that your Teddy might have fleas, visually inspect the fur all the way to the skin. A bad flea infestation will leave behind "flea dirt," tiny black flakes from your dog's itchy skin. Even if you don't see any dirt, run a fine-toothed flea comb through your Teddy's fur. You'll see live fleas caught squirming in the bristles if there are any to catch.

The other thing about fleas is that they don't just afflict your dog. They can get all over your house, living in cracks and laying eggs that lie dormant only to give forth their offspring just when you think you've wiped them out. I have never experienced this sort of infestation, but some people have to go so far as to have their house "bombed" with flea-killing chemicals by a pest control company. It's much better (and easier) to keep fleas off your pup from the start.

I won't recommend any specific brands here, and all brands aren't available in every market anyway. Suffice it to say, I have found it prudent to splurge for an all-in-one flea/tick/heartworm/roundworm/hookworm treatment. It works wonders, only has to be applied every couple of months, and is simple and effective. These treatments are usually liquid-filled pouches that, when opened, are emptied onto your dog's skin between the shoulder blades. Here, even a wiggly puppy can't reach the stuff and lick it off, leaving it to do its work. The formula is absorbed into the skin and works one of two ways. One sort kills the fleas as soon as they take their next bite (this is the kind I like). The other makes the current fleas infertile, effectively killing off the next generation of parasites. Both have been deemed safe for dogs, and your vet will be able to give you exactly the amount of product you need for your tiny puppy.

Pill-form medications are available to quickly stop bad infestations. These are available from your vet as well. They aren't a permanent solution, but if you ever find your dog in a bad way with fleas, needing fast relief, this sort of treatment is appropriate.

Ticks are an even nastier parasite. They start out as tiny, flat, black creatures, the size and shape of the head of a small tack. But once latched on to a blood source, they can swell to the size of grapes. They are very prominent on the east coast of the United States, and the diseases they carry are even worse than those spread by fleas. Lyme disease is considered by some to be an epidemic in some climates of the United States. Not only that; it is easily spread to humans, even if the tick rode in on your dog. Ticks carry other dangerous, but less common, diseases as well.

Tick protection is absolutely essential if your dog goes into green, natural spaces at all, specifically forests and overgrown areas. They are treated very much like the fleas in the examples above. If your puppy or other dogs are currently untreated, it is best to check them for ticks after hikes and other outdoor excursions. Ticks favor moist, hidden places on the body: around the ears, the tail, the abdomen, and legs. If you live in a tick-prone area, check the dog's skin while wearing gloves. If you find a tick, flush it, treat the bite with an antibiotic cream, and wash your hands. Keep an eye on the dog and call your vet about any potential concerns for ticks in your area.

Other common dogs' parasites, like ear mites and mites that cause mange, can also be treated in all-in-one formulas like the ones that fight fleas and ticks. These infestations can get really bad without attention, but they don't have to give your dog trouble at all, provided you take action against them before they start.

Worms and Internal Parasites

Internal parasites are a scary thought, but there's no need to worry. Your vet will examine your pup's stool at its first checkup. The stool will be tested for parasites and their eggs, with results available in hours or a few days. It is not at all uncommon for a new puppy to have worms. Tiny puppies will often eat anything in sight. They can also pick up worms and other parasites this way. If your puppy has some of these parasites, he will be treated at the vet's office. Puppies tend to be a little groggy after this treatment, but the issue is typically resolved simply. In some cases, a second treatment may be necessary.

Dogs can get all kinds of internal parasites, affecting different body systems. Some worms, like hookworms, stick to the gut. They can even live there without causing problems, simply living off of food that is being digested. This doesn't necessarily mean that you want them there, but they are really nothing to fear in small numbers. The worms you absolutely want to avoid are heartworms. These parasites, as you might expect, live in the heart itself. Unchecked, they can populate so vigorously that they actually clog the heart. This typically occurs only in adult dogs that have been severely neglected. When treating dogs like this, the dog must be kept still for a couple of days even after the worms are killed, because the worms can cause a heart attack before being expelled. Your Teddy Bear will be tested occasionally throughout its lifetime for heartworms and other parasites, receiving easy treatments before any of these parasites become a problem.

Benefits of Veterinarians

Every dog should have a veterinarian. These doctors are highly trained specialists. They know dozens or even hundreds of dogs in your area. Consequently, they know what illnesses might be going around. They know what illness looks like, no easy thing with tiny animals that can't speak for themselves. And they know how to treat it.

Look around for a vet who makes you feel secure and who your puppy seems comfortable with. Prices can vary amazingly, depending on the area where your vet's office is located. After a move to a new city last year, I tried out 4 different vets before settling on one that was a good fit for my animals.

Veterinarians can also give you great advice. We like to think that everything that can be learned about dogs is available on the internet, but that's really not true. Dogs are living beings. They change, have unique personalities, and need individual care. By establishing a good relationship with a local veterinarian, you will have a second pair of eyes watching your puppy grow. A good vet can clear up questions you might have about feeding, exercise, and any potential concerns. They're also the one you call if your pup ever has an emergency at 3 AM. A good veterinarian is an indispensable part of your Teddy Bear's long, healthy life.

Holistic and Home Remedies

There are many, many home remedies for common puppy problems like fleas and earaches. We'll cover just a few here. Always consult a veterinarian if problems are ongoing after home or holistic alternatives.

Homemade Flea Bath. Does your Teddy have a few fleas? Here is a great way to clean them off and discourage new ones from hopping on. In two cups of warm water, mix half a cup of fresh lemon juice and half a cup of your normal puppy shampoo. Lather your pup from head to toe with this mixture and allow it to sit for a minute. Then rinse liberally with warm water, and watch the little black parasites circle the drain. I like to follow this treatment with a gentle flea-combing to catch any stragglers. To kill these clingers-on, I boil some water and dip my brush in to kill fleas caught in its bristles.

Fleas can also be discouraged by putting a few drops of lavender and cedar oil onto a moist handkerchief. Tie this around your pup's neck for walks in outdoorsy places, where fleas can lurk. An extra drop by Teddy's tail will help protect the hindquarters.

Outdoor Tick Boots. Most ticks latch onto people and dogs at their feet. Then they make the long climb to groins and armpits where they make their home. Humans keep ticks at bay by wearing socks in the woods, but puppies often remain unprotected. Take baby socks and secure them around your pup's paws, up to about the knee joint. This will give ticks no flesh to grab onto and will keep your dog from picking up most of them.

Cleaning Ears. If your puppy is scratching or rubbing its ears, or if the ears appear fire engine red inside, you likely have an ear infection on your hands. Painful ear infections are best treated by a vet, but you can keep ears clean to clear up minor irritations. Take a cup of water, two cups of white vinegar, and a teaspoon of rubbing alcohol. Put this into a squirt bottle and gently squeeze a little into the ear canal. Wait for a minute or two, then wipe away the wax and liquid slurry that is left over. Never reach into the ear canal. Just get the stuff that comes out. A solution like this will dissolve waxes that have hardened deeper in the ear. Repeat this as needed, but only if your pup's ears aren't red and painful.

Diet and Bathing for Skin Itches and Allergies. For pups prone to itchy skin, sometimes the best thing is a quick soak in cool water. Skin problems can become aggravating. The puppy will itch and, in scratching to make the itch go away, irritate the area more. By intervening with a soothing, cool bath, you can help stop the itch before it is exacerbated.

For allergies, consider improving the quality of the pup's food. Eliminate all grains, and consider a protein source other than chicken if chicken is in your current food. Some research suggests that chicken can irritate the skin of certain dogs, but this is controversial. Finally, add some milled flax seed or liquid fish oil to the pup's kibble. These omega oils will do wonders for itchy skin.

There are many alternative dog health options out there. Most of them are expensive and provide dubious benefit to your pet, at best. The keys to a dog's health and well-being are simple. A puppy needs love and leadership, good food, exercise, and a safe place to live. Health care helps ensure that all of these facets are in order, and supplements them with care and treatment if necessary. Alternatives, especially among unlicensed practitioners, are often more expensive than they are effective. Never give your dog medications that are unregulated or untested. Herbal and vitamin supplements may be a good addition to your dog's diet, but these should be checked out by your vet. Finally, acupuncture, Reiki, and massage are all available for your dog. They may even do some good, but I would urge you to use careful judgment before signing up your pup, especially if the price is worrisome.

The one alternative practice that I have seen work wonders for a dog is chiropractic. However, this tends to be a good option only from dogs suffering from age- or weight-related pain and immobility, or injury. Your new puppy won't have any of these problems, and won't need these services any time soon, if at all.

Vaccinating Your Teddy

Vaccinations are also completely essential. Puppies derive immune protection from their mothers, but this wears off after 6 to 8 weeks. For this reason, puppies should be vaccinated immediately if you are bringing them home shortly after weaning. Some breeders will have the first round of vaccines taken care of before you pick up your Teddy pup. This will be clearly communicated, and you can schedule the rest of your pup's vaccine schedule with your vet accordingly.

We all remember childhood vaccinations. Those were no fun at all. Fortunately for your pup, lots of immunizations can be delivered from a single shot. At your Teddy's initial doctor's visit, it will be given a shot to protect against:

- **Canine Distemper Virus** - This virus is contagious, and there is no cure. Your pup should be protected before it has the chance to catch it.

- **Hepatitis** - Another virus, which also afflicts humans, and damages the liver.

- **Leptospirosis** - This is a bacterial illness that hurts puppies' kidneys. It can also be picked up by many other animals and humans.

- **Parainfluenza** - This is a virus that will give a puppy a terrible and dangerous cough resulting from upper respiratory infections.

- **Parvovirus** - This is a terrible disease mainly afflicting puppies and old dogs. The virus lives in the ground. Once caught, the disease is very painful and usually fatal. I have seen its effects, and it is an awful disease, but it is easily prevented with early vaccination.

- **Coronavirus** - It has similar symptoms to Parvo (above), but it won't usually kill a puppy. It will, however, make it very sick and cause an awful mess.

In order to get the jump on all these nasties, be in touch with your vet before you bring your puppy home. He or she can tell you exactly when to bring the dog in. Don't forget the stool sample! If you are visiting a new vet after having one round of vaccinations at another office, make sure to bring those records with you, or have them emailed/faxed ahead of time.

Your vet will tell you exactly what vaccination schedule you need to follow with your Teddy, but they usually work something like this:

• 6-8 weeks: the first combination vaccine, as described above.

• 9 weeks: a second booster vaccine.

• 12 weeks: another booster. Ask about the need for a Lyme disease inoculation at this point.

• 16 weeks: the final booster shot. Your pup is covered for life. Your Teddy will also be vaccinated for rabies at about this time.

Once your puppy has these basic vaccines, your vet visits will grow much more infrequent. Always remember to make these visits as fun and comfortable as possible. Some dogs actually like going to the vet. They get treats. They get attention from nice people. Give your pup an extra special something to munch on at the doctor's office, and your Teddy may have fun while getting protected from all of these illnesses.

CHAPTER 16

ADVANCED TEDDY BEAR HEALTH

Because a Teddy Bear puppy is a 50/50 mix of two purebred parents, one Bichon Frisé and one Shih Tzu, your puppy will have some of the health characteristics of both breeds. However, because of its mixed heritage, your puppy will also benefit from the genetic combination, avoiding most of the breed-specific ailments that frequently pop up in either parent breed. Because some of these nagging breed problems get eliminated in mixed offspring, Teddy Bears also tend to live longer than either parent dog breed. It is not uncommon for these dogs to live between 15 and 20 years, or even more. For these reasons, new owners should expect many years of robust health from these sturdy little dogs. But there are still health issues that crop up, as they do in all aging animals. We'll go over some Teddy-specific ailments, and the common diseases of their parent breeds, below.

Common Diseases and Conditions

Epilepsy, breathing problems, and deafness are uncommon illnesses in Teddy Bears, but are reported often enough to bear mentioning. It should be noted that because Teddy Bears are a newer designer breed, there simply isn't the wealth of data that long-standing breeds like Shih Tzus have. As there is always a chance that a trait may be passed on for either parent, common diseases among Tzus and Bichons are listed as well.

Epilepsy

While more common in large dogs, seizures affect all breeds to varying degrees. Seizures are not a big problem for Shih Tzus or Bichon Frisés, though they may occur. Seizures can have many causes, but they are most commonly identified as a genetically inherited trait. Many times, the cause is unknown. Symptoms typically manifest in puppies of around 6 months to 2-3 years old. Symptoms may persist into adulthood, occur in clusters with long gaps in between, and may be successfully stifled with medication.

Seizures can be distressing to witness, and they are certainly a scary and confusing time for a dog. The dog may paw the air, convulse, drool, and whine. But typical seizures are not life-threatening. They will run their course in little over a minute. The dog will appear dazed and confused for a couple of minutes following an attack, but will soon act like nothing ever happened. Your Teddy Bear is unlikely to exhibit epileptic symptoms, but if he does, get appropriate medication from your veterinarian. Also avoid dangerous situations like swimming, where a sudden seizure could cause drowning.

One note: salty dog treats often contain potassium bromide, an epileptic trigger. If your dog has epileptic seizures, eliminate these treats from its diet and ask your vet about medication that regulates potassium bromide levels in the blood.

Breathing Problems

This trait may be inherited from a Teddy's Shih Tzu parent. Shih Tzus have short snouts. When properly bred, their small noses are often no bother, but some individuals still have trouble breathing. Small-snouted or flat-faced dogs may also have elongated palates, narrow nasal passages, and collapsed voice boxes. As a result, these dogs will wheeze, snore, cough, and snort. They can also have trouble eating and drinking, and are susceptible to overheating and heat exhaustion. These problems are not nearly as common in Bichon Frisés.

In order to ensure that your Teddy Bear pup won't have this problem, meet the parent dogs if you can. At least, ask your breeder if this is a problem in any of their puppies, or for a history of breathing and other health problems in their adult Shih Tzus. Breathing problems aren't universal to Shih Tzus, and a reputable breeder will not breed any dogs who are likely to pass undesirable or dangerous congenital health problems on to their offspring.

If you do happen to have a Teddy Bear with breathing problems related to any of the causes above, the problem is not life-threatening. Your vet can examine a puppy to make sure that no hazardous conditions are present. The main thing to do is avoid prolonged exposure to heat and humidity. Due to their decreased ability to pant away body heat, heat exhaustion can overwhelm small dogs with breathing difficulties. Beyond that, you will enjoy your wheezy, but otherwise normal, Teddy Bear.

Deafness

Deafness is not at all common in Teddy Bear puppies. At this age, the problem would be considered congenital, and no respected breeder sells a deaf puppy as if it were a healthy one. Congenital deafness in Teddy Bear puppies is almost never seen, however. If you do find yourself with a deaf Teddy pup, contact your breeder and discuss your options. You may be entitled to a partial refund or veterinary bill assistance.

Though you certainly want a Teddy Bear that can hear, deafness is no impediment to an otherwise happy and healthy life. Deaf dogs still make excellent pets. Deafness that develops with age, as it does with many dogs, is sometimes even treatable. Hearing loss can be the result of inflammation within the ear, and this is the case for most Teddies that are totally or partially deaf. Sometimes hearing can be somewhat restored with the reduction of the inflammation, as swelling lets up and normal drainage is resumed.

By keeping your pup's ears clean and healthy, you will go a long way in preventing deafness in the future. Ask your vet about routine ear cleanings. A veterinarian may recommend occasional hair plucking from the ears to prevent wax/crud buildup and to stave off ear infection. Ear mites can also give way to inflammation that causes deafness. If your puppy frequently scratches its ears, or if they appear red inside, have your vet take a look. Whether from allergies, parasites, infection, or blockage, your pup's ears should always be kept clean and clear. This way, your Teddy will have a much better chance of keeping its sharp hearing for the rest of its life.

Common Shih Tzu Diseases

Shih Tzus can suffer from most of the health afflictions experienced by other small dogs. They also have some unique maladies of their own.

Eye, Teeth, and Breathing Problems

These various issues are all caused by the Shih Tzu's small head. Because of its small mouth, the Shih Tzu's teeth can be crowded and crooked. They also emerge later and fall out earlier than the teeth of other breeds.

Similarly, the small cranium and flat face of a Shih Tzu can cause their eyes to bulge. The bug-eyed appearance is to be expected to some extent, but too much bulge can result in blood loss to certain eye tissue. Unchecked, this will result in blindness. Finally, the aforementioned breathing problems sometimes found in Teddy Bears dogs, are much more common in Shih Tzus.

Though these concerns are somewhat frequent, they are by no means present in every dog. A good breeder will have eliminated these concerns. He or she will also be able to give you a specific history of their animals' health problems and testing. If a breeder does not provide detailed health information for their dogs, buy from someone who does. A small head and flat face are desirable traits in Shih Tzus. It is what gives them their characteristic appearance. But in trying to achieve the breed standard traits, breeders may go too far, resulting in animals with unhealthy cranial exaggerations.

Patellar Luxation

Shih Tzus' kneecaps can pop out of place. They may refit themselves naturally, or the dog may need veterinary attention. If a joint is especially prone to disconnect, the joint may become inflamed and arthritic. This is another problem that should not be present in a healthy Shih Tzu.

Renal Dysplasia

This is a problem with kidney development. The condition is usually inherited from the parents, but a Shih Tzu may demonstrate symptoms of renal dysplasia spontaneously. A good breeder will not breed adult Shih Tzus that have this disease. The signs of renal dysplasia in an otherwise healthy dog are constant thirst, lack of weight gain, and a general appearance of weakness or malaise.

Other Eye Problems

In addition to the eye problems resulting from bulge, listed above, Shih Tzus may also have dry eyes (from too little tear production), cataracts, and progressive retinal atrophy (PRA), which results in blindness. Dry eyes can be treated with drops and even simple surgery, if necessary. PRA is not typically treatable, but cataracts can be removed with a simple surgery.

In addition to these somewhat common eye problems, Shih Tzus have been known to experience ingrown eyelashes. These can lead to ulcers within the eyeball or even slightly puncture the eye surface. The symptoms of this would be evident with pain, discomfort, and pawing at the affected eye by the dog.

Other issues

Shih Tzus may also suffer from misalignment of the spine, liver disease, and obesity. Obesity contributes to the development of many other diseases and discomforts, especially diabetes. Not all of these can be counted out by the dutiful care of a good breeder, but animals that are the offspring of healthy parents will be much more likely to be healthy themselves. Since you are likely interested in the puppies of a Shih Tzu and a Bichon Frisé, ask to see both of the parent dogs. If there are health defects present in one or the other, these may very well be eliminated in their offspring, but it is much better if they are never in the mix in the first place. It is expected, of course, that breeders will be willing to provide health information about both parents. Don't accept any less.

Common Bichon Frisé Diseases

Like Shih Tzus, a healthy Bichon Frisé is a long-lived small dog, happy and free from major health concerns for most of its life. However, some health problems, when present, afflict Bichon Frisés disproportionately compared to other breeds. Some of these concerns are shared with Shih Tzus and other small breeds; others are more common to Bichons.

Bladder Problems

It is not uncommon to see bladder infections and bladder stones in Bichons. An infection is typically the first problem. As inflammation develops, stones begin to form, and before you know it, the dog has a very painful problem. The stones result from a diet too rich in protein, magnesium, and phosphorus. They may also form if a Bichon has to wait too long to urinate. In any case, possible bladder infections should be examined by a vet quickly. If treated for infection, painful bladder stones can often be avoided. Some bladder stones may be passed naturally, but others will be too large to remove without surgery. Prevention is all the more attractive with this consideration.

Allergies

The Bichon Frisé is known for being somewhat prone to allergies. Allergies occur when the body's infection-fighting cells attack healthy body tissue while trying to neutralize perceived threats, like pollen and certain foods. Bichons may be allergic to environmental factors, food ingredients, and flea bites. Fleas are especially nettlesome to Bichons, but are easily prevented or eliminated with routine treatments. Even one flea bite can cause a Bichon to break out all around the affected area.

Patellar Luxation

This kneecap misalignment is as described in the Shih Tzu information above. It is not uncommon in small dogs and may need veterinary attention to prevent later dislocation and the threat of arthritis.

Sensitivity to Vaccination

Nearly all dogs feel somewhat unwell soon after receiving vaccinations, but Bichon Frisés do so more frequently. They may experience hives, exhaustion, swelling, and other symptoms in the hours and days following one of these injections. While this discomfort is no reason to forgo vaccinations, these puppies should be watched carefully to make sure they have no serious problems following vaccines. This sensitivity is similar to the dogs' reaction to flea bites and other allergens. Any foreign body or substance is tough on them.

Hip Dysplasia

This painful health problem is typically associated with larger dogs, not the sprightly Bichon. But it can still occur, the result of the hip bone being malformed and unable to fit snugly in its socket. Arthritis can develop around the affected joint, causing pain and eventual lameness. By ensuring that previous generations are unaffected, a Bichon Frisé buyer can be relatively sure that a new puppy won't develop this condition.

Cataracts

These can occur on the eyes of any dog, and can be removed with surgery, but cataracts can be found in unusually young Bichon Frisés (< 6 years). This condition is typically found to be hereditary, like many of the others listed.

Final Thoughts

With Teddy Bear health, it's the little things that count. By consistently applying sound principles in raising your new puppy, health concerns will not have to weigh on your mind (or your bank account). I've covered some of these points before, but I'll sum it up here for your convenience:

❶ **Buy From a Good Breeder** - Because Teddies are a popular breed right now (and because they are so darn cute), many breeders are offering them to the public. Some of these operate their businesses without good breeding, health, and sanitation practices in place. Their puppies may be inexpensive, but they also might have nagging health problems as they age. When you buy from shady breeders, you support the practice and set yourself up for lots of future veterinary costs. Make the investment for a pup from a reputable breeder. After all, this animal may be with you for the next two decades!

❷ **Vaccinate, Train, and Socialize from the Start.** By vaccinating properly from a very young age, you get a jump on the nasty diseases that can really hurt a Teddy pup. By training and socializing, you'll have a young dog that understands important commands that could save its life in an emergency. The dog will also understand how to act around other people and animals, making it a better friend to all. Also, don't neglect to get your pup spayed or neutered at a time scheduled with your veterinarian. Veterinary care and mentally stimulating exercise will go a long way in growing your puppy right, and will set good patterns for future health.

❸ **Proper Food and Continued Activity.** Make sure your puppy has access to the right amount of good food throughout life. Proper nutrition will stave off many of the illnesses that plague dogs around the world. A properly fed and exercised dog is much more likely to live without arthritis, diabetes, obesity, cataracts, allergies, and so much more.

❹ **Safety, Consistency, and Love.** When your dog feels secure, he will be at his best. When you train, play with, and lead your Teddy with consistency, he will feel secure in his role in your pack. He will know he has a part to play and he will enjoy fulfilling it. Above all, just love the little dog. Your love will help you make the best choices, giving your puppy a long, healthy life.

CHAPTER 17

YOUR AGING TEDDY BEAR

Teddy Bears are healthy and long-lived. These little dogs typically live to be 15 or 16, with some living past 20. But no dog lives forever. By preparing for your pup's old age, you will make sure that the final years are as healthy and happy as possible. You'll be able to avoid many of the illnesses and injuries that plague aging dogs. Long-time Teddy Bear owners know the value of a mature dog. It has lived with you for years. It is calm and dependable. Dog and master share a special bond. Even if you have a Teddy pup only a few weeks old, you have a lot to look forward to in its adult and senior years.

Senior Dog Care

Old Teddies go at a different pace than younger dogs. They will also need more advanced care from your veterinarian. You will need to focus more on diet than you have in the past, as obesity becomes more of an issue in older dogs. An aging dog may also become more prone to parasites and infections, due to a slowing immune system. It may have more difficulty getting around than before. Your dog may need help with long staircases and jumping up onto the bed. Make sure they always have access to food and water and a comfortable bed to sleep on. And most importantly, make sure your old Teddy feels loved and valued just like it did when it was a puppy.

Fortunately for the Teddy Bear owner, Teddies don't age as "hard" as larger breeds. This is a general statement, and individual aging will vary, but Teddies typically maintain health and mobility until their last few weeks or months of life. It is not uncommon for a decline in health to occur abruptly, shortly before they pass on or are put to sleep. Long, healthy years are one of Teddy Bears' best features, but it makes the final days all the sadder. We'll take a deeper look below at all of the considerations you should make for your aging Teddy.

Grooming

The most important grooming factors for an aging Teddy are cleanliness and comfort. These involve bathing, combing, hair cutting, and the removal/prevention of mats. Teddies have an advantage in their senior years. Because they are so small, any owner can easily move them around, keeping them bathed and clean. This process is much more difficult with an aging Golden Retriever, for instance, but the tiny, totable Teddy is no trouble at all. What is more, Teddies tend to stay active well into their advanced years. They simply don't present the challenge that larger senior dogs do.

If your Teddy does lose mobility in its later years, you will still be able to care for it. Bathe the dog gently and keep the hair brushed and cut. No old dog will look like a puppy forever, but don't just let the coat get overgrown. You may find that you are able to keep your Teddy's fur cut as you like it on your own. Even if you were reliant on a groomer during your dog's younger years, you will likely be able to maintain its coat with scissors and an electric razor as the years go by. Other owners like to keep up routine groomings as long as their dogs are able. I believe that dogs derive confidence from feeling that they look good, even if it is just from the attention given during groomings. It can be therapeutic for an older Teddy Bear.

The most important factor to keep up is brushing. Because older Teddies sleep and lie around a little more than younger dogs, they are more prone to mats, especially if not regularly brushed. Their long, wavy hair can easily lock into a messy tangle called a mat. These mats may "hover" above the skin, or may go all the way to the hair roots. The mats aren't simply uncomfortable for the dog. They can also deprive the skin of oxygen, hold on to moisture, and be a hotbed for infection and inflammation. Some dogs get "bed sores" and "hot spots" beneath large mats. So don't let your aging Teddy's fur get messy. Clean and brush your old pup regularly.

Nutrition

As stated above, you Teddy will likely age more slowly than larger dogs. Even so, its nutrition requirements will change with time. If you notice your aging Teddy sleeping more and running around less, it will have lower caloric needs than a more active dog. At this point, you should start feeding the dog a lighter kibble. Many manufacturers supply food specifically for older dogs, with carbohydrate and protein level optimized for the more mature dog's needs.

Another thing to consider is dental health. It is important to maintain a dog's teeth at all ages. Veterinarians can give your Teddy periodic dental cleanings through all stages of life. This will keep the teeth clean and in place for as long as possible, to ensure that your Teddy can break apart the food you give it. If your older dog has lost some teeth, consider a soft food that is easily chewed and swallowed, or soften the dog's kibble with water or broth.

Old Teddies need more fiber to maintain regular bowel movements, so look for this in any food that you give a senior dog. Also avoid the extra calories found in some dog treats. Find a healthy snack that your dog loves, like an apple slice, or lower-calorie treats available at pet stores. By keeping your older Teddy from packing on the pounds, you will rule out many late in life diseases, like diabetes, that cause older dogs' health to quickly decline.

Finally, make sure that your aging Teddy remains adequately hydrated. Dehydration is a problem for small dogs in general, and all the more so as they get older. By adding some moist or wet dog food to your Teddy's diet, you'll make sure that it is getting all the water it needs. If your dog tends to restrict its activity to one or two areas of the house, have water available in both spaces. Some older dogs won't make the trip all the way downstairs to get a drink, even if they're thirsty.

Exercise

Teddy Bears are plucky dogs. They tend to stay active, looking for adventure and stimulation as long as they live. But they do lose a step or two once they get above the age of 10 or so. If your Teddy is turning into a couch potato, don't let it become totally sedentary. Your older dog won't need to spend quite as much time running around as it used to, but keep up the walking and play schedule that you have maintained for its entire life. By doing so, you'll keep up your older dog's musculature, circulation, and mental acuity. Old dogs tend to decline much faster when there is a sudden cessation of their activity.

Most Teddies tend to want to keep going until they are very old. You will see virtually undiminished enthusiasm when you pull out the leash and the waste bags. If you let your Teddy off leash in a dog park type scenario, make sure that the play doesn't exceed its ability to participate. Younger, rougher dogs can fluster and overwhelm and aging Teddy. Some older dogs enjoy going to these places, without getting too caught up in the action. Many will be perfectly happy just sitting with you, watching the other dogs romp. If your dog likes this, keep up the visits to the dog park, as a kind of social stimulation, but don't let the dog get in over its head recreationally. Of course, if your older Teddy can still run around with the young pups, don't prevent this.

Mental Stimulation

Dogs are social animals. I spoke about this briefly in the previous paragraph. Play is a very important part of your Teddy's life. It is how it learns, motivates itself, exercises, and feels like a part of a social group. It is not uncommon for old dogs to become "shut-ins". Because of their declining energy and risk of health problems, some owners will keep older dogs in the house, still and quiet. Sometimes this can start if an older dog is recovering from an injury. The owner will simply forget to bring the dog back into the world of walks and play that it previously enjoyed. Play is especially important in the recovery process for older dogs, after surgeries and convalescence. Keep him moving, and you may be surprised at how well your Teddy bounces back.

You should also keep your Teddy's mind active by presenting new challenges. Make sure the dog remembers previous training, and teach new skills. It isn't true that you can't teach an old dog new tricks. In fact, it's a very healthy form of exercise for them, keeping them in the game, so to speak. If your Teddy feels like it has a job, even if that job is just to find the leash, it will feel much more motivation to stay active and engaged with the life of your family. If your dog feels retired, it will be much more prone to depression and the onset of many senior health concerns.

Regular Vet Exams

After the age of 10, your Teddy's veterinary visits should become more frequent. A young, healthy dog in the prime of its life may go more than a year without seeing the inside of a vet's office. But older dogs should maintain at least yearly checkups. The focus of these visits will be to correct any specific health concerns, and to identify potential difficulties before they become emergencies.

You should ask your vet about your Teddy's weight and food. Most Teddies stay trim through their adult lives, but if your dog is tipping the scales, make sure that the weight isn't excessive or dangerous. Typically teddies don't weigh more than 12 or 13 pounds. This should be true at all ages. Make sure that the food you are feeding your dog is appropriate. Your vet will probably be familiar with any brand you can name. If unfamiliar with your brand of choice, he or she can easily decode the ingredients list on the back of the bag, or evaluate your homemade senior Teddy food.

You vet should check your older Teddy's hips, ears, and teeth. Teeth can be maintained throughout life, but may begin to fall out in very old Teddies, owing to their Shih Tzu heritage. Ears can also be kept clean and healthy throughout life using methods described earlier. Finally, hips can begin to fit more loosely in their sockets with age. This isn't always the result of genetics or poor breeding. In older dogs, muscles simply become weaker. The muscles that hold the hip in place may not keep it fitted tightly. As stated earlier, this isn't as big a problem in Teddies as it is with larger dogs, but nonetheless your animal doctor should check. Hip dysplasia can give way to arthritis and immobility.

Ask if your dog's exercise schedule is adequate. Exercise can both exhaust and invigorate aging dogs, and your Vet will have a sense of this. Sometimes these little dogs have more energy than they can handle, as they get older. Some would benefit from being still just a little more. Have your Teddy's blood and urine checked for a number of issues. In older dogs, your vet will be looking for hormone and nutritional deficiencies as well as signs of diabetes or infections. If any problems turn up, ask your vet about the possible need for supplements in your older dog's diet.

Finally, have your vet give your Teddy the once-over for tumors. Benign fatty tumors are very common in old dogs, and are even found in younger dogs. These aren't to be worried about unless they grow too large. In very old dogs, there may be cancerous growths that will not develop enough to endanger their lives before they pass from other causes. Your vet will be able to spot these growths ahead of time, recommend further testing, or recommend that no action be taken.

Hopefully, by this time, your vet is a trusted friend, familiar with your Teddy Bear for many years. A vet like this will be able to spot sudden health changes in your dog, directing you to important corrections and treatments.

Common Old Age Ailments

Many of these issues have been discussed already in this and the previous chapter. Arthritis, diabetes, cancer, and blindness can sometimes be prevented and treated. Other times, no doctor can eliminate them. Some of these are very likely to be present in the life of a Teddy Bear that lives more than 12 or 15 years.

Other age-related illnesses common to dogs of all kinds are kidney disease, gum disease, and dementia. Kidney disease, if uncorrectable, is often a sign of the end. The body is no longer able to eliminate waste products as it once did, and your dog will feel very unwell for it. Gum disease is not as serious and is sometimes correctable, at least preventable. It is possible for gum disease to progress past the limits of surgical repair or your budget. As always, it is best to use preventative methods to keep ailments like this from developing in the first place. Finally, dementia is not uncommon in older dogs. These dogs become confused, sometimes irritable and unpredictable. They may need extra help getting out to use the bathroom, finding their food, and feeling safe. If dementia is paired with blindness or deafness, normal life can be very confusing for an aging Teddy. If they are otherwise healthy, treat them with extra compassion to make them as comfortable and happy as possible.

Enjoying the Final Years

Teddy Bear dogs have some of the best health of any breed during the senior years. But they don't last forever. As such, even brand new owners should occasionally think about the days when their Teddy will grow old and die. A dog of advanced age has had many years with you. It will be well trained and totally adjusted to your personality and your way of life. You will love each other quite a lot. Mature and senior Teddies are still affectionate and cuddly, but a little calmer and a little more steady. For some, they have become the perfect pets.

If your Teddy Bear's health is declining, it is important to objectively evaluate their quality of life. The Quality of Life Scale (or HHHHHMM scale) helps saddened owners figure out how much pain and trouble their dog feels on a daily basis as they advance in age. Owners score their pets on a scale of 1 to 10 regarding Hurt, Hunger, Hydration, Hygiene, Happiness, Mobility, and More Good Days Than Bad. With a score of 35 or higher, a dog is healthy enough to be enjoying life with its family. But when the score dips below 35, it is time to consider putting the animal to sleep. Many devoted dogs will hang on for longer than they should. The euthanasia or "putting to sleep" process is peaceful and painless. While it is difficult for owners to make this decision about their old friends, it is the best choice for dogs that have lived long, full lives.

I think it's especially wonderful to care for a dog for its entire life, from puppyhood to old age. You get to watch your dog grow and mature, with lots of joy and laughter along the way. You also get to provide a wonderful life for your little friend. You have a life outside of your home: your work, your friends, your interests. But for your dog, you are their entire life. They wait for you when you are away. They love you more than anything. This love is undiminished in a dog's older years, and your Teddy will be no exception. He deserves the same love and nurturing that he has been given throughout his life.

CHAPTER 18

TRAVELING WITH TEDDY BEAR PUPPIES

There are many advantages of owning a small dog like a Teddy Bear. Small dogs fit in a wider variety of living situations. They comply with size and weight ordinances for housing complexes, hotels, and other "pet friendly with exceptions" venues.

Small dogs eat less than big dogs and they usually make smaller messes - a huge benefit for many potential owners. They require less exercise and for the most part small dogs are completely happy being adored as lap dogs. They will sit contently and watch television or snuggle under the blankets for a good, long nap. Small dogs are just easier to add to a household regardless of the size of the family.

As a part of a human family, a small dog is more transportable that bigger dogs. A Teddy Bear puppy will stow in a soft tote for anything from a walk in the park to a shopping excursion, to a fashion show. If properly trained, a Teddy Bear can go nearly anywhere its human travels.

Dog Carriers

Since Teddy Bears will have an average adult weight of 10 pounds or so, transporting your dog will be a stress-free task. Size and weight aside, it is important to consider safety first when traveling with your dog. Do you need to use a carrier? If so, what kind is best?

There are hundreds of different crates, bags, totes, and purses designed for traveling with your dog. Owners of small dogs have an abundance of choices. You can spend a lot of money purchasing a jewel encrusted, designer travel bag, or you can stick to the basics of a molded carrier.

To save time and money, the first step in determining the appropriate doggie travel device is to consider the means of transportation. Will you be walking, riding a bike, or taking a car or bus? Perhaps your travel will involve trains or airplanes. The choice of carrier may depend on how you will be moving.

To suit the vehicle there are several basic types of carriers to accommodate travel with a Teddy Bear:

• Hard-sided, molded carriers

• Wire crates

• Purses/totes

• Other soft-sided carriers

• Strollers and sliders

• Slings and front packs

When your decision is made regarding the type of carrier, the next step is to determine the size. You must make sure any carrier is suitable in size and construction for your precious cargo. Measure your dog and select a size that fits his or her physical requirements.

The most important measurements to consider are the height and length of the dog. Weight is only important as a guideline for the restrictions of the transportation mode. Measure the height from the floor to the top of dogs withers (front shoulders). Next, measure the length from the neck to the tip of the tail.

• Hard-sided, molded carriers and wire crates should be three to five inches longer and higher than the length and height measurement of your dog. The dog should be able to stand and lay comfortably in the crate. If the size of the carrier recommended for your dog provides less than three inches clearance in length or height, purchase the next larger size.

• Soft-sided carriers should be two to three inches higher and longer than the dog.

• Purses and totes should add at least one inch for clearance to your dog's height and length.

• For slings and front packs, make sure there is enough room to hold your dog comfortably but not enough of a gap for her to slip out

• Strollers should be large enough to provide for your dog's comfort without gaps for her to slip through.

Car Rides

Teddy Bear dogs love car rides. Most are always ready for anything from a run to the corner store to a cross-country trip. Some precautions for car safety are necessary to protect your puppy and to obey traffic laws.

Several states have passed motor vehicle legislation requiring safety restraints for animals transported in cars and trucks. Depending on where you are driving, failure to restrain or crate your dog could make you subject to fines and/or other penalties. In any case, it is not a good idea to allow your dog freedom in a moving vehicle. It is dangerous for the pet, for the people in the car, and for the vehicles you may meet on the road.

Accidents are usually the result of one second of carelessness. Practice common sense, obey your state's laws, and remember to:

• Buckle children and pets in the back seat for maximum safety

• Use approved safety devices (crates and safety harnesses)

• Never become distracted by pets or other passengers

• NEVER let an animal ride on the lap of a driver

• Make sure that every passenger in a moving vehicle wears a safety restraint

NEVER leave a dog unattended in a hot car. A dog can suffer a heat stroke in as little as 10 minutes!

Hotel Stays

The U.S. census reports that nearly 43 million households in the country have at least one dog. It is reasonable to assume that many people also travel with their pets. Teddy Bear dogs are small, compact, and easy to pack up and take along. So as you travel with your pup, look for and patronize the more than 100,000 hotels and motels in the country that welcome pets.

Pet-friendly lodging was once very difficult to find. Today, with so many pets considered family members, it is necessary for hotels and motels to establish a pet-friendly status to remain competitive. Some chains charge a fee for pets and most will hold a refundable security deposit for any damages. There are also limitations on size, weight, and breed, and restrictions on the number of pets per guest room to consider.

When staying at a hotel or motel with your dog you are guests. Overnight establishments permit you the opportunity to stay with your pet as a courtesy - not an obligation. Be respectful of the lodging and of other guests. Walk your dog only in designated areas, pick up any debris they leave, and deposit waste bags in proper receptacles. Do not allow your dog to bark all night, disturbing other guests. If possible, keep your dog crated while in the hotel room.

Online sites like Dogfriendly.com publishes a travel guide listing pet-friendly hotels, restaurants, and other establishments by state and country.

If you are going to stay in a hotel during your holiday travels, plan ahead. Check with the reservation agents or look at pet policies for specific hotel chains on the Internet. Lodging establishments and restaurants are required to observe the service dog protection laws under ADA.

Local hotels may have individual policies regarding pets. Respect the rules and other guests. Walk your dog only in designated areas. Clean up any debris your dog leaves behind and dispose of it properly. Keep him quiet and crated when possible. Hotels allow pets as a guest courtesy-not an obligation. By practicing good pet conduct those considerations are much more likely to continue.

Flying with Your Teddy Bear

Airlines provide for three different types of transport for dogs:

• Passenger cabin travel
• Excess baggage travel
• Cargo travel

Regardless of the type of airline travel you plan for your dog, you must book a reservation. Do not show up at the ticket counter with your dog and expect to put him or her on the plane.

Passenger cabin travel - all airline carriers limit the number of animals in the passenger cabin on a single flight. Tickets for pets are offered on a first come, first served basis by reservation. There are restrictions for weight (about 15 pounds or less), and animals must fit in an approved, soft carrier. Most airlines require that a pet in the passenger cabin remain stowed under the passenger's seat at all times. Carry-on pets must be ticketed - fees vary.

Excess baggage travel - if your dog is traveling on the same flight with you, he may be checked at the gate as excess baggage. Fees are usually dependent on the size and weight of the animal. Reservations for pets are required and an airline-approved crate is mandatory. Pets traveling as excess baggage should have a water source in the crate. Unless otherwise posted, the pet may be collected at the oversized luggage area of baggage claim.

Cargo travel - this option must be used for airline travel if your dog is not traveling on the same flight with you. Animals traveling in cargo transport are subject to the same guidelines as those traveling as excess baggage. Dogs must be confined to airline-approved crates with a drinking water source. Drop-off and pick-up locations for cargo travel vary from airport to airport. A reservation for the pet traveling in cargo transport is required.

Airlines are prohibited by federal law from transporting live animals as excess baggage or as cargo if the pet is exposed to temperatures that are below 45° F or above 85° F for more than 4 hours upon arrival, departure or during connecting flights.

A certificate of health that includes rabies and up-to-date vaccinations is required for air travel. The document must be issued by a licensed veterinarian no more than 10 days prior to transport. Most countries require periods of quarantine before they will release your pet for travel within the country. Very clear owner information (name, address, phone number, destination address, emergency contacts) should be visible on the outside of the crate and included on the inside of the container.

Kennels

There may be occasions when traveling with your dog is not possible. In these cases, it becomes necessary to find caregivers for your pet. One option is boarding your Teddy Bear in a kennel.

Kennels, like every other pet product, have come a long way in the last decade. Indulgent owners have options for doggie boutique hotels and spas to canine camps complete with arts and crafts, campfires, and other activities. Gone are the days of chain link runs and outdoor pens.

If you are considering boarding your pet at a kennel there are a few tips to make the separation and stay as pleasant for both parties as possible.

Get recommendations and references - talk to friends, neighbors, and coworkers to find the best boarding facility.

Visit and inspect the facility - does the kennel appear clean? Are the dogs comfortable and properly cared for? Do the dogs have individual sleeping quarters and runs?

Meet the staff - do the employees seem kind and knowledgeable? Do they like the animals?

Health standards - does the kennel require proof of vaccinations for boarding? Do not leave your pet in a facility that does not meet basic health certifications, including requiring vaccinations for rabies and canine kennel cough (Bordetella).

Walking the dog - boarding kennels should provide a minimum number of minutes for exercise a day.

Separate but equal - are the cats and dogs segregated?

Food - can you bring your dog's food?

Medications - will the kennel staff administer medications? Is there an extra fee for the service?

Emergency aid - is an emergency veterinarian available to residents? Check references to make sure.

Understand the fee schedule - discuss base fees and additional charges for special services such as: individual playtime, swimming lessons, closed circuit, distance monitoring, special treats, administering medications, and grooming. The tab can run up quickly with a la carte services.

Reserve a room early - plan your pet's stay as soon as possible especially around busy holiday seasons. Top quality kennels fill up quickly.

Boarding your dog at a kennel is a great socialization opportunity. Some dogs do not adjust well, and responsible kennel operators will turn away young puppies and senior dogs who have never been boarded. While it is better to leave your dog in a setting with other people and animals, the stress of a busy new environment may be too much. If you are considering using a kennel, take your dog in for half day visits to evaluate his response and acclimation to the setting.

House/Pet Sitter

Hiring a house/pet sitter is another option if you must leave your dog for extended periods. House/pet sitters may be more expensive than a boarding kennel, but your dog will receive specialized attention in his own home. The familiar surroundings will minimize the stress of separation.

House/pet sitters come with a variety of skill levels. You may interview your neighbor's teenage son to sit with your dog, or you may prefer a professional service. Either way, make sure you provide a checklist of responsibilities and expectations.

If you are looking for a professional house/pet sitter you may start with your veterinarian's office for a referral. Two nationally recognized companies; the National Association of Pet Sitters (NAPS) and Pet Sitters International have a directory of certified house/pet sitters. The agencies provide referrals by city. Most registered professional sitters have a license and certification credentials and must pass criminal background checks.

Don't be afraid to discuss fees which may range up to $100 per day depending on the services. Have the sitter come by a few days in advance to get acquainted with your dog and the household routine. Review the list of emergency contacts. A good sitter understands you worry about your beloved pet. They will send updates and as a bonus-pictures!

Train and Bus travel

If your holiday plans include transporting your pet by bus or train, you may begin to consider other arrangements! Amtrak does not permit animals on any of their trains (there are exceptions for service animals protected by the Americans with Disabilities Act).

Bus travel is equally restricted for those with pets. Bus companies that travel interstate are prohibited from transporting pets, although these policies exempt service dogs. Local bus and commuter lines including subways running service from airports establish their own pet policies.

If you are going to depend on bus or train service during your trip, make a call to the carrier you will use to confirm the rules for your pet.

Automobiles

The best way to transport your pet by car is in a crate. It is safe and actually will provide the animal with a higher level of security. In the event of an accident or during a pit stop the dog will not accidentally escape.

Add a favorite toy to the crate with a comfortable mat. Give the dog a break during stops, along with a drink of water. Depending on the length of the trip, you may consider withholding food until you reach the day's destination.

If your dog isn't a seasoned car traveler you may want to take a few short road trips with her before the holiday drive. She will acclimate to the motion and routine much better when travel days arrive. Your veterinarian can also prescribe tranquilizers or recommend antinausea treatments.

Keep the vehicle adequately ventilated. NEVER let a dog hang his head out of the car window. It is dangerous and can lead to eye, ears or nose injuries. NEVER let your dog ride in the back of an open pickup truck.

A Few Good Tips

- Fit your dog with a good, sturdy leash, collar, harness, and, if indicated, muzzle for travel. Remember that he is going into unknown territory and may be frightened. Practice safety for your animal, yourself, and your fellow travelers.

• Check collars for updated identification and rabies tags. Some jurisdictions will fine pet owners for walking dogs in public places without rabies verifications.

• Pack medications, food, bowls, and bottled water.

• Make a pet safety check of the environment where you and your dog are staying. Look out for hazards such as exposed electric cords, garbage cans, plants, ornaments, wrapping paper and ribbons, toys, and anything your dog may eat!

If you plan to board your pet, make reservations early! Kennels fill up fast during the holidays. Have current rabies and vaccination records. Most kennels will not board a sick animal or a female dog in heat.

With a little planning and preparation the holidays - even the traveling - will be fun-filled and stress-free for you and your Teddy Bear!

Made in the USA
Middletown, DE
30 March 2016